# SOHRAB AND RUSTUM

## AND OTHER POEMS

MATTHEW ARNOLD'S

# SOHRAB AND RUSTUM

AND OTHER POEMS

EDITED

WITH NOTES AND AN INTRODUCTION

BY

ASHLEY H. THORNDIKE, Ph.D., L.H.D.
PROFESSOR OF ENGLISH IN COLUMBIA UNIVERSITY

Fredonia Books
Amsterdam, The Netherlands

Sohrab and Rustum and Other Poems

by
Matthew Arnold

Introduction and Notes by Ashley H. Thorndike

ISBN: 1-58963-929-4

Copyright © 2002 by Fredonia Books

Reprinted from the 1910 edition

Fredonia Books
Amsterdam, The Netherlands
http://www.fredoniabooks.com

All rights reserved, including the right to reproduce this book, or portions thereof, in any form.

In order to make original editions of historical works available to scholars at an economical price, this facsimile of the original edition of 1910 is reproduced from the best available copy and has been digitally enhanced to improve legibility, but the text remains unaltered to retain historical authenticity.

# CONTENTS

| | PAGE |
|---|---|
| INTRODUCTION | vii |
| Arnold's Life | vii |
| Arnold's Poetry | xi |
| Sohrab and Rustum | xv |
| BIBLIOGRAPHICAL NOTE | xxiii |
| CHRONOLOGICAL TABLE | xxiv |
| SOHRAB AND RUSTUM | 3 |
| SELECTED POEMS: | |
| QUIET WORK | 31 |
| SHAKESPEARE | 31 |
| REQUIESCAT | 32 |
| THE FORSAKEN MERMAN | 33 |
| SWITZERLAND | 37 |
|     Meeting | 37 |
|     Isolation. To Marguerite | 38 |
|     To Marguerite—*Continued* | 39 |
| PHILOMELA | 40 |
| DOVER BEACH | 42 |
| BACCHANALIA; or, The New Age | 43 |
| SELF-DEPENDENCE | 47 |
| A SUMMER NIGHT | 48 |
| LINES WRITTEN IN KENSINGTON GARDENS | 51 |
| THE FUTURE | 53 |
| THE SCHOLAR-GIPSY | 56 |
| THYRSIS | 64 |
| MEMORIAL VERSES | 72 |
| A SOUTHERN NIGHT | 75 |
| RUGBY CHAPEL | 80 |
| CALLICLES'S SONG | 87 |
| NOTES | 89 |

# INTRODUCTION

### ARNOLD'S LIFE

MATTHEW ARNOLD'S poetry was written largely during his early manhood, most of his prose after he was forty years old. His life as a man of letters is consequently divided into two nearly distinct parts. The 1867 volume of poems virtually completed his poetry; the lectures "On Translating Homer," published in 1861, began his work as a critic and writer of prose.

The eldest son of Dr. Thomas Arnold, the famous headmaster of Rugby School, he was born December 24, 1822, at Laleham, England. Six years later his father went to Rugby, which Matthew entered as a pupil in 1837. He was successful there as a student; and he graduated with distinction at Oxford in 1844, where among other honors he won the Newdigate prize with a poem on Cromwell. He then taught a while at Rugby, and in 1847 became private secretary to the Marquis of Lansdowne, who was in charge of the administration of public education. In 1851, he married Miss Frances Lucy Wightman, and in the same year became Lay Inspector of Schools. To the work of this post he gave the larger portion of his time and energies until his resignation in 1886. Much of his work was sheer drudgery, but he gave himself heartily to the task of improving and extending the public school system, and his studies and reports of schools on the continent were of importance in promoting the changes which he desired.

In 1849, Arnold published a small volume entitled "The Strayed Reveller and Other Poems," which he shortly withdrew from circulation. In 1852, another volume, "Empedocles on Etna and Other Poems," containing among others his "Tristram and Iseult," failed to attract any attention. In 1853 appeared a third volume, containing the best of the earlier poems, excepting "Empedocles on Etna," and in addition two of his longest poems, "Sohrab and Rustum" and "The Scholar-Gipsy." This volume won some recognition from the public, and new editions were issued in 1854 and 1857. In 1855, Arnold published a second collection of his poems, including "Balder Dead," like "Sohrab and Rustum," a narrative in blank verse. In 1857, he was elected professor of poetry at Oxford, a position which did not require residence, but only occasional lectures. In 1858, appeared his "Merope," a tragedy on the Greek model; and in 1867, the year in which his professorship ended, a volume of "New Poems." This contained the beautiful elegies, "Thyrsis," "A Southern Night," and "Rugby Chapel." Henceforth he wrote only a few poems as special occasions called for them.

To the 1853 volume of poems Arnold prefixed a preface, which urged that English poetry should return to classical simplicity and serenity. This, his first essay at criticism, was a declaration of the principles which he always maintained. His Oxford lectures resulted, in 1861, in a volume "On Translating Homer;" and from this time on, prose volumes on various subjects followed almost yearly. Of these the most enduring in their value are undoubtedly those dealing with literary criticism. In that field no book has since appeared of equal importance with the "Essays in Criticism" (1865). Arnold's criticism is important in at least three main directions: (1) In indicating the functions and insisting on the need of literary criticism, especially in English literature; (2) In appreciative and discriminating valuations of the writers whom he liked; (3) In formulating principles and tests for the right appreciation of literature. Although Arnold's taste was not very catholic, and although he was too disdainful of exact knowledge and could even write on subjects about which he knew little, as in the case of Celtic literature, and although he pressed his rules and formulas too hard; yet, since Coleridge and Hazlitt, no literary criticism in English is comparable with his either in its influence on popular opinion or in its permanent value.

The range of his other prose writings is great. Arnold had set himself to the task of criticism not merely of literature but of the English people,—of their politics, their religion, their institutions, their ideas,—in short, of their civilization.

In a letter of 1863 he wrote to his mother: "It is very animating to think that one at last has a chance of *getting at* the English public. Such a public as it is, and such a work as one wants to do with it!" And in an earlier letter of the same year he wrote: "However, one cannot change English ideas so much as, if I live, I hope to change them, without saying imperturbably what one thinks and making a good many people uncomfortable. The great thing is to speak without a particle of vice, malice, or rancour." These quotations indicate clearly the purpose of Arnold's prose and the qualities which he consciously sought. He was fighting for a cause, and he intended to make people uncomfortable, but he hoped to reform English life by writing without rancor and with entire imperturbability.

## INTRODUCTION

Several volumes deal specifically with education. Others discuss questions of religious belief, interpretation of the Bible, and the policy of the church. Others, as "Friendship's Garland" (1871) have to do with political questions. Still others set forth Arnold's theories and principles as applied less to special fields than to the national life in general. The most important of these is "Culture and Anarchy" (1867), which accuses the British middle class of inaccessibility to ideas, narrowness and conventionality of morals, disregard of art and beauty, and of an absorption in commercial and industrial organization and advance. These qualities Arnold grouped under the general name "Philistinism;" and to them he opposed his doctrine of "Culture," the gospel of "sweetness and light," "the impulse to the development of the whole man, to connecting and harmonizing all parts of him, perfecting all, leaving none to take their chance." Culture is to be judged and fostered by Criticism, '"a disinterested endeavor to learn and propagate the best that is known and thought in the world." This is not the place for a discussion of Arnold's doctrines and his applications of them; but it must be noted that, though he aroused much irritation and opposition, he succeeded in his purpose of making the public listen to him, and that his prose work has been of marked influence on English thought during the past fifty years. Like Carlyle, Ruskin, and Emerson before him, he made literature a means for urging the reform of our civilization and persuading men to a higher valuation of the world of reason, imagination, and spirit.

Arnold's life continued a busy one, even after a pension permitted a retirement from the inspectorship of schools in 1886. In 1883-4, he lectured in the United States, where his eldest daughter married, and where he visited

## INTRODUCTION xi

again in 1886. He wrote frequently for magazines, and edited volumes of selections from Dr. Johnson, Wordsworth, Byron, Burke, and from his own poems. At the height of his reputation he died suddenly, on April 15, 1888, and was buried in the churchyard of All Saints, Laleham. Arnold was devoted to his family, from which he derived great happiness, despite the loss of three children. Among his friends he was much beloved. Among the many tributes to his life and character, Mr. William Watson's poem "In Laleham Churchyard" should be remembered; and Lord Morley's lofty praise:

"He was incapable of sacrificing the smallest interest of anybody to his own; he had not a spark of envy or jealousy; he stood well aloof from all the hustlings and jostlings by which selfish men push on; he bore life's disappointments—and he was disappointed in some reasonable hopes—with good nature and fortitude; he cast no burden upon others, and never shrank from bearing his own share of the daily load to the last ounce of it; he took the deepest, sincerest, and most active interest in the well-being of his country and his countrymen."

### ARNOLD'S POETRY

ARNOLD'S prose was devoted to specific criticism and to definite ideas, the results of a carefully considered view of life. His poetry came earlier, before he had reached fixed conclusions, and presents not settled theories and principles but rather his struggle toward belief and his effort to find right principles of living. Consequently, it reflects varying and unsettled moods, and is in part a record of unrest and questioning.

Like other poets of the Victorian era, he was facing a new age. The industrial revolution of the preceding half-century had brought into existence the world of huge cities, of factories and tenements, railways and the telegraph. The kind of existence which is represented by a great manufacturing city of to-day was new, and it brought strange and difficult problems for men to solve. To a greater extent than any former epoch, the new age seemed given over to industrialism and commercialism; to buying and selling, to building larger, travelling faster, and spending more than ever before. Things that are lovely and of good report seemed neglected and forgotten in the rush and excitement of commercial progress. Meantime there had been almost as much change and ferment in the world of thought as in the world of industry. The ideas which were represented by the French Revolution still threatened to overturn and transform church, state, and society; and in Arnold's own lifetime the new and far-reaching discoveries in natural science made further demands for changes in traditional and long established modes of thought. In philosophy, in politics, in social theory, in every field of intellectual activity, and most of all in theology and religion, men were questioning and attacking old views and seeking new. In his poetry, Arnold was forever facing the conditions and problems of the new age, but ever looking back wistfully at virtues or ideals of the past, which the present seemed hastening to relinquish. He was in quest of religious truth, in search of something that might give a firm resting place for facts and reason, and a renewed assurance for noble and unselfish living. He turned to the Greeks for aid, and to nature with its calm serenity, and to modern teachers like Carlyle and Emerson, and still more to the great men of the preceding generation, Goethe, Byron, and Wordsworth; and he pleaded for the qualities which afterwards played a large part in his doctrine of culture—for disinterested service, for moderation and dignity, for self-dependence and resignation. But his poetry never quite attains the calm it praises, and still less does it attain the assurance and imperturbability of his prose.

Though Arnold's poetry came to reflect his own moods and those of an age of disturbed faiths, yet this was by no means the purpose and ideal which he set for poetry. In his preface to the 1853 volume of poems, containing "Sohrab and Rustum," he opposed current tendencies in English poetry. He criticized as characteristically English defects, the "taste for brilliant phrases and isolated felicities, and the want of attention to unity and consistency." He asked, "What are the eternal objects of Poetry, among all nations and at all times?" and answered, "They are actions, human actions; possessing an inherent interest in themselves, and which are to be communicated in an interesting manner by the art of the Poet." He further insisted on the importance of a noble and worthy subject, adding "that the Greeks understood this far better than we do" and that they were also the masters of "the grand style." Arnold's positions are open to attack, but he remained loyal to them in both his poetry and his criticism of poetry. Henceforth, in practice and theory, he was ever the exponent of simplicity and dignity of style, of nobility and unity in subject. His models were Homer and the Greek tragic writers, and the English poets who came nearest to these in "the grand style"—Wordsworth, Gray, and Milton. His poems, entirely apart from their subject matter, have consequently a special value and charm in that they carry on the great classical tradition in literature, a tradition rarely better exemplified than in his "Sohrab and Rustum."

His poems, all of which can be contained in a moderate

sized volume, fall into a few main divisions. The Lyrics, which constitute the first division, are mostly expressive of moods of religious questioning and of moral resolution; and they have had a special appeal for the last two generations of readers who have known mental experiences similar to Arnold's. Among the best and most characteristic are "Dover Beach" and "A Summer Night." The second class, the Elegies, gave Arnold an opportunity to praise what seemed highest and best in the men he commemorated. The chief elegies, "Rugby Chapel," "A Southern Night," "The Scholar-Gipsy" and "Thyrsis," are his consummate poetic work; and they exhibit sentiments more positive and less troubled than the lyrics. The third group consists of two dramatic poems, which represent his closest imitation of the Greeks. The fourth group, the narrative poems, vary greatly in subject matter and treatment. In these, however, Arnold had an opportunity to escape from himself and the troubles of his age, an opportunity to devote his poetry to the narration of noble and pathetic stories in a way not unworthy of the great masters of verse. And he was by no means forbidden the introduction of modern sentiment. The two poems generally considered the best of this class, are "The Forsaken Merman" and "Sohrab and Rustum." They attain high excellence with very different subjects and by very different means.

Arnold's poetic fame grew slowly. His earliest volumes made no impression on the public, and his best work gained scant popular approval in comparison with Tennyson and Browning, or indeed with other poets of the time. His literary criticism had no such rivals to fear and won a quicker success, while his other prose writings attracted attention because of their contemporary interest and controversial character. During the last twenty-five years of his life, as we have seen, he assumed the position of general censor of the English people, so it naturally became a commonplace to assert that in him the critical temperament predominated over the creative and poetical. But the poems live on and widen their circle of readers; and, as much of the prose loses its interest with the passage of time, Arnold the poet is receiving justice in the contest with Arnold the critic. His productiveness was not great, nor his range wide, but in his chosen fields few English poets have equalled him.

## SOHRAB AND RUSTUM

"Sohrab and Rustum" was written and published in 1853. In May of that year Arnold wrote to his mother: "All my spare time has been spent on a poem which I have just finished, and which I think by far the best thing I have yet done, and I think it will be generally liked; though one can never be sure of this. I have had the greatest pleasure, in composing it, a rare thing with me, and, as I think, a good test of the pleasure what you write is likely to afford to others. But the story is a very noble and excellent one."

Rustum, who is supposed to have lived some time before Cyrus the Great, is a famous Persian hero, and the story of his encounter with his son is the best known episode in the "Shah-Namah," or Book of Kings, the national epic of Persia, written by the poet Firdusi about 1000 A.D. Parts were translated into English by James Atkinson, in his "Sohrab, a Poem" (1814). Arnold quoted in his notes the following summary of the episode from Sir John Malcolm's "History of Persia:"

## INTRODUCTION

"The young Sohrab was the fruit of one of Rustum's early amours. He had left his mother, and sought fame under the banners of Afrasiab, whose armies he commanded, and soon obtained a renown beyond that of all contemporary heroes but his father. He had carried death and dismay into the ranks and had terrified the boldest warriors of that country, before Rustum encountered him, which at last that hero resolved to do, under a feigned name. They met three times. The first time they parted by mutual consent, though Sohrab had the advantage; the second, the youth obtained a victory, but granted life to his unknown father; the third was fatal to Sohrab, who, when writhing in the pangs of death, warned his conqueror to shun the vengeance that is inspired by parental woes, and bade him dread the rage of the mighty Rustum, who must soon learn that he had slain his son Sohrab. These words, we are told, were as death to the aged hero; and when he recovered from a trance, he called in despair for proofs of what Sohrab had said. The afflicted and dying youth tore open his mail, and showed his father a seal which his mother had placed on his arm when she discovered to him the secret of his birth, and bade him seek his father. The sight of his own signet rendered Rustum quite frantic; he cursed himself, attempting to put an end to his existence, and was only prevented by the efforts of his expiring son. After Sohrab's death, he burnt his tents and all his goods, and carried the corpse to Seistan, where it was interred; the army of Turan was, agreeably to the last request of Sohrab, permitted to cross the Oxus unmolested. To reconcile us to the improbability of this tale, we are informed that Rustum could have no idea his son was in existence. The mother of Sohrab had written to him her child was a daughter, fearing to lose her darling infant if she revealed the truth; and Rustum, as before stated, fought under a feigned name, an usage not uncommon in chivalrous combats of those days."

From Malcolm's history, Arnold took names and references to other of Rustum's many exploits. But in choosing the story for his poem, his first care was to separate this particular episode from the other events of the national epic, and then to remove some matters connected with it in the Persian narrative. In the interest of unity, he omitted the beautiful account of the frantic grief of Sohrab's mother, which takes much space in the Persian poem, and he greatly shortened the combat, which lasts three days in the original. He omitted also accounts of prowess at arms, and he added the crucial incident of the father's cry of *Rustum!* which so moves the filial affection of Sohrab that he lowers his guard and meets his death. The interest of the story is thus entirely centred in the emotions of father and son. The story thus condensed and integrated, is a simple though a moving one. It offers a chance for good characterization and dramatic dialogue, and it requires some descriptive passages to provide the proper atmosphere and background. To these descriptions of nature, Arnold gave much more space than the original poem. He also added, after the manner of Homer, many similes—some of them very elaborate—thus increasing the poetical beauty and dignity of the story.

The setting for the story is two-fold. We are made to see the camps and armies and the combat by "the broad Oxus and the glittering sands," and we are also made to feel that the events belong to a time and land remote from ours, to a vast realm stretching from the mountains of Central Asia to the Aral Sea, a land of famous cities, many peoples, and mighty deeds. The atmosphere for the story comes partly from the specific descriptions and partly from the geographical allusions. The geographical names, frequent here as in Homer and Milton, are used sometimes for their rhythmical effect, but they also help to create a mental vision to serve as a framework for the sad life of Sohrab.

The poem opens with the morning sun breaking the fogs over the Oxus, and closes with a magnificent description of the mighty river flowing on, all unmindful of the tragedy enacted on its border. The Oxus, now called Amu Daria, rises in the high tableland of Pamere (Pamir) in Turkestan, and flows 1300 miles, forming the northeastern boundary of ancient Persia, and emptying at last through a delta, "shorn and parcelled," into the Aral Sea. Near the delta are Kipchak, Orgunjè, and the more important Khiva. To the north of the river is Turkestan and its great cities, Samarcand and Bokhara. To the north and west, were the homes of the Tartar hosts, on the plains of the Jaxartes, which, like the Oxus, emptied into the Aral Sea; and north of the Aral Sea, the steppes of the Kuzzaks (Cossacks) and the plains of Kirzhiz. South of the Oxus was Persia, and we hear of its cities and ancient capital Persepolis. Far to the west on the eastern shore of the Caspian Sea, was Ader-baijan, the home of Sohrab's mother; and far to the east in Afghanistan, was Seistan the realm of Rustum. A study of a good atlas will make clear most of the geography of the poem; the details are unimportant, but perhaps one's pleasure in reading is increased if one knows the general relations of these rivers, mountains, and cities with their strange, verse-filling names.

Arnold's use of the Homeric simile in this poem has

## INTRODUCTION xix

sometimes been criticised as excessive and artificial. Be this as it may, the similes undoubtedly add much to the picturesqueness of the story. Some of them are modern, but the large majority are in keeping with the manners and habits of the time of the story, and many of them make in themselves clear-cut and memorable pictures in our minds. The file of cranes streaming over Casbin (l. 111 ff.), the troop of pedlars from Cabool (l. 160 ff.), the wet diver from the Persian Gulf (l. 284 ff.), the young cypress in a queen's secluded garden (l. 314 ff.), the single tower in the desert (l. 337 ff.), the unlopp'd trunk fished from the flooded Hydaspes (l. 409 ff.), the eagle circling above his eyry (l. 556 ff.), the shepherd who descries "a far, bright city smitten by the sun" (l. 620 ff.), the cunning workman in Pekin (l. 672 ff.), and those black granite pillars in Persepolis (l. 860 ff.):—all these create for us pictures of the Asia of long ago and help us to realise the scenes in which Sohrab and Rustum lived. And not less beautiful are some of the simpler figures: the shiver through the field of grain (l. 156), the hyacinth lying in the mown grass (l. 634 ff.), or "the soil'd tissue of white violets" (l. 844 ff.). The similes everywhere aid in making impressions from the verse vivid, sensuous, and delightful. They seize our attention with some unexpected picture and so relieve the tension of the painful story.

The poem is written in blank verse (unrhymed iambic pentameter). Its divisions into paragraphs, indicated as in prose by the indention of the first word, should be carefully noted by the student. The verse is modelled on Milton's, and the lists of geographical names and the elaborate similes recall Milton as well as Homer. Arnold in the main sought for purity rather than richness of style. He did not, like Shakespeare or Browning, mass figure on figure with reckless profusion; nor did he, like Keats or Tennyson, seek to give each detail a rich decorative value. He aimed at simplicity, propriety, and dignity of diction. If he wished for ornamentation, he made a single, carefully-wrought simile; if he found the right word or phrase, he did not hesitate to repeat it. The repetition of words is, indeed, one of the most striking stylistic peculiarities of the poem. Sometimes the repetition serves for emphasis, sometimes it knits passages firmly together. Sometimes it becomes a mannerism, a too-frequent rhetorical device. One trick, which Arnold perhaps caught from Milton, he is especially fond of—the echo of a phrase with a slight addition or change. There are many instances of this in the poem; as,

> But now in blood and battles was my youth,
> And full of blood and battles is my age. (ll. 824-5.)

> but the grave is cold!
> Heaven's air is better than the cold dead grave.
> (ll. 323-4.)

Occasionally the verse may seem overstudied, but everywhere it shows how carefully Arnold was working for the Greek virtues of clarity, restraint, and succinctness.

The poem has often been said to approach closely to Greek models partly because of its attainment in a large measure of these qualities, and partly because of the character of its story, and the directness of its appeal to primitive human feelings. It is, however, surely a mistake to think that the poem's resemblance to the Greeks is very close. While Arnold was imitating Homer, he had, as we have seen, English models as well; and there is much in the poem that is neither Homeric, nor Greek, nor primitive. The dwelling on emotions is not Homeric; the invention of Sohrab's unnerving at his father's shout of *Rustum* is a modern refinement; and the great speeches, though touched with a fatalism and dignity worthy of an early heroic age, are touched too by the sentiments of the nineteenth century. Arnold would have been the first to deprecate a comparison of the poem with the great passages in the Iliad which come closest to it in theme. He was fond of declaring that such passages as the farewell between Hector and Andromache, the combat between Hector and Achilles, and the interview of Priam and Achilles are the consummate and unmatchable triumphs of narrative poetry. It may be added that they are different from modern narratives in other respects than that of excellence. They record a state of society far less complex than ours, and they simplify emotions in a way that no modern is likely to do. What may be fairly said of Arnold's poem is that he succeeded better than any other poet in telling a story in English blank verse in a manner resembling Homer's. The poem is, however, far from being merely an imitation of Homer or of anyone else. It is rather one of the best representatives in English of those principles which have distinguished the greatest masterpieces of epic poetry.

Its diction has already been contrasted with that of other poets. The contrast might be extended to the plan and structure and all the elements of the artistic treatment. Tennyson's "Idyls of the King" also retell old stories of war and sorrow, and he sentimentalized and moralized the stories and gave them an abundance of poetic decoration. Browning also retold old stories, and made them expressive of his individual philosophy, or illustrative of some unusual or striking human motives, and he was especially successful in his depiction of moments of intense dramatic stress. Arnold took an old story, simplified it rather than elaborated it; and, while he added some modern sentiment and intensified the dramatic crisis, he restrained himself from much moralizing, or decoration, or expression of individual opinion. He strove merely to give the noble and pathetic story the harmonious and beautiful expression which it deserved. This is not to say that he is a better poet than Tennyson or Browning, but it is to say that here he has aims and methods different from those which are usually theirs.

There are many kinds of poetry, many effects which it can produce, and many ideals toward which it may strive; and the range of its appeal to human emotions widens with each generation. "Sohrab and Rustum" represents only one kind of poetry, the epic; and is only an episode, not a full epic. It represents no effort to give a comprehensive view of human life or a profound and searching study of human character; it represents an effort to tell a story impressively. In this effort it certainly succeeds. If from its limitations it is not to be compared with Milton or Homer, it may yet serve as a standard of poetic excellence and a touchstone for poetic taste. Anyone who cares for Homer will find much to admire here. And, whether one cares for the Greeks or not, he will find in "Sohrab and Rustum" an example of unity and harmony of conception and of simplicity and dignity of expression that should guide him to an appreciation of one of the great ideals of poetry, which has enlarged and inspired men's minds ever since it was so nearly realized by Homer.

# BIBLIOGRAPHICAL NOTE

UNIFORM editions of Arnold's works are readily obtainable. A one volume edition of his poems is published by the Macmillan Company. Two volumes of his letters were published in 1895 under the editorship of Mr. G. W. E. Russell. A good bibliography of his writings by T. B. Smart appeared in 1892. Three critical biographies are in existence, one by Professor Saintsbury in *Modern English Writers* (1899), one by Mr. Herbert Paul, in the *English Men of Letters* (1902), and one by Mr. G. W. E. Russell, in *Literary Lives* (1904). No one of these is an entirely satisfactory Life. There have also been numerous essays and studies. Among those dealing especially with his poetry may be mentioned "Victorian Poets," by E. C. Stedman, 1885; "The Greater Victorian Poets," by Hugh Walker, 1895; "Matthew Arnold," by W. H. Dawson, 1904; and essays by George E. Woodberry, *Warner's Library;* T. H. Ward, "Ward's English Poets," vol. IV, enlarged edition; Augustine Birrell, "Res Judicatæ;" W. E. Henley, "Views and Reviews;" A. C. Swinburne, "Essays and Studies;" R. H. Hutton, "Essays Theological and Literary," vol. II; Andrew Lang, *Century Magazine*, 1881. Two or three of the best essays on his prose writings are by Frederic Harrison ("Tennyson, Ruskin, Mill," etc.); W. C. Brownell, "Victorian Prose Masters;" L. E. Gates, "Three Studies in Literature;" J. M. Robertson, "Modern Humanists;" W. H. Dawson, "Matthew Arnold and his Relation to the Thought of his Time," 1904.

# CHRONOLOGICAL TABLE

| Arnold's Life and Works. | Contemporary Literature and History. |
|---|---|
| 1822. Dec. 24. Born at Laleham. | 1822. Shelley died. Pasteur born.<br>1824. Byron died.<br>1825. Huxley born. Macaulay's Essay on Milton.<br>1828. George Meredith and D. G. Rossetti born.<br>1830. Opening of the Liverpool and Manchester Railway. Tennyson: Poems, chiefly lyrical.<br>1831. Hegel died. Poe: The Raven. Whittier: Legends of New England.<br>1832. Reform Bill passed. Scott and Goethe died.<br>1833. Carlyle: Sartor Resartus. Browning: Pauline. Tennyson: Poems. Balzac: Eugénie Grandet.<br>1834. Coleridge and Lamb died. Dickens: Sketches by Boz. Balzac: Père Goriot. |
| 1837. Entered Rugby School. | 1837. Victoria became queen. Swinburne born. Thackeray: Yellow-plush Papers. Dickens: Pickwick (begun in 1836). Carlyle: French Revolution.<br>1838. First steamship crossed the Atlantic.<br>1839. Longfellow: Hyperion. |
| 1840. Alaric at Rome, Rugby prize poem.<br>1841. Entered Baliol College, Oxford. | 1840. Thomas Hardy born. Penny Post established.<br><br>1842. Dr. Arnold died. Tennyson: Poems. Macaulay: Lays of Ancient Rome. |

| Arnold's Life and Works. | Contemporary Literature and History. |
|---|---|
| 1843. Won Newdigate prize with poem on Cromwell. | 1843. Wordsworth poet-laureate on the death of Southey. Ruskin: Modern Painters (vol. i). Dickens: Christmas Carol. |
| 1844. Graduated from Oxford. | 1844. Telegraphy invented. Dumas: Trois Mousquetaires. Thackeray: Barry Lyndon. |
| 1845. Elected to a fellowship at Oriel College. | 1845. Mexican War. Secession of J. H. Newman from the Church of England. Browning: Dramatic Romances and Lyrics. Hawthorne: Mosses from an Old Manse. |
| | 1846. Repeal of the Corn Laws. Marian Evans (George Eliot): Translation of Strauss's Life of Jesus. |
| 1847. Became private secretary to the Marquis of Lansdowne. | 1847. Tennyson: The Princess. Longfellow: Evangeline. Thackeray: Vanity Fair. C. Brontë: Jane Eyre. |
| | 1848. Revolution in France; abdication of Louis Philippe; Louis Napoleon, Prince President of the French Republic. Insurrections in Austria, Hungary, Italy, Poland, Prussia, Spain, and other countries. Great Chartist meeting at Kensington. Gold discovered in California. A. H. Clough: Bothie of Toberna-Vuolich. Macaulay: History of England (vols. i. and ii.). |
| 1849. The Strayed Reveller and other poems. | 1849. Dickens: David Copperfield (finished 1850). Emerson: Representative Men. Sainte-Beuve: Causeries du Lundi begun. |
| | 1850. Wordsworth and Balzac died. Tennyson becomes poet laureate. Mrs. Browning: Sonnets from the Portuguese. Tennyson: In Memoriam. Hawthorne: Scarlet Letter. |

| Arnold's Life and Works | Contemporary Literature and History. |
|---|---|
| 1851. Appointed inspector of schools. Married Miss Frances Lucy Wightman. | 1851. Exhibition at the Crystal Palace. |
| 1852. Empedocles on Etna and other poems, including Tristram and Iseult. | 1852. Napoleon III Emperor of France. Thackeray: Henry Esmond. |
| 1853. Poems, a new edition including Sohrab and Rustum and The Scholar-Gipsy. New editions in 1854 and 1857. | 1853. C. Kingsley: Hypatia. Mommsen: Römische Geschichte (vol. i.). |
| | 1854. Crimean War. Treaties of Japan with England and United States. Thackeray: The Newcomes (begun). |
| 1855. Poems, including Balder Dead | 1855. Fall of Sebastopol. Browning: Men and Women. Tennyson: Maud. Longfellow: Hiawatha. |
| | 1856. Heine died. Mrs. Browning: Aurora Leigh. |
| 1857. Appointed professor of poetry at Oxford. | 1857. Indian Mutiny. First Atlantic Cable. Compte and De Musset died. Buckle: History of Civilization. Trollope: Barchester Towers. Flaubert: Madame Bovary. |
| 1858. Merope. | 1858. Carlyle: History of Frederick the Great (vols. i. and ii.). George Eliot: Scenes of Clerical Life. Gladstone: Studies on Homer. W. Morris: Defence of Guinevere. Tennyson: Idyls of the King (first and incompleted form). Holmes: Autocrat of the Breakfast Table. |
| 1859. England and the Italian Question. | 1859. Macaulay and De Quincey died. Darwin: Origin of Species. Dickens: Tale of Two Cities. George Eliot: Adam Bede. G. Meredith: Richard Feverel. E. Fitzgerald: Translation of Omar Khayyam. |

| Arnold's Life and Works. | Contemporary Literature and History. |
|---|---|
| 1861. Popular Education in France.<br>On Translating Homer. | 1861. William I. King of Prussia; Bismarck his chief minister. Victor Emmanuel, King of Italy. Inauguration of Lincoln; Secession of the Confederate States. Mrs. Browning died. George Eliot: Silas Marner. C. Reade: The Cloister and the Hearth. |
| | 1862. Herbert Spencer: First Principles. George Meredith: Poems and Ballads. C. Rosetti: Goblin Market and other poems. |
| | 1863. Gettysburg; Surrender of Vicksburg. Thackeray died. George Eliot: Romola. Huxley: Man's Place in Nature. Tyndall: Heat as a Mode of Motion. Renan: Vie de Jésus. |
| 1864. A French Eton. | 1864 Landor died. Browning: Dramatis Personæ. Cardinal Newman: Apologia pro Vita Sua. Swinburne: Atalanta in Calydon. Tennyson: Enoch Arden. |
| 1865. Essays in Criticism. | 1865. End of Civil War and assassination of President Lincoln. G. Meredith: Rhoda Fleming. Ruskin: Sesame and Lillies. Whittier: Maud Muller. Carlyle: Frederick the Great, finished. |
| | 1866. North German Confederation formed. Gladstone's Reform Bill. Swinburne: Poems and Ballads. |
| 1867. Finished his second term as professor of poetry at Oxford. New Poems, including Thyrsis, A Southern Night, and Rugby Chapel. On Study of Celtic Literature. | 1867. Disraeli's Reform Bill passed. |

| Arnold's Life and Works. | Contemporary Literature and History. |
|---|---|
| 1868. Schools and Universities on the Continent. | 1868. Browning: Ring and the Book. W. Morris: Earthly Paradise (vols. i. and ii.) |
| 1869. Culture and Anarchy. Collected Poems, 2 vols.; new editions, 1877, 1885. | 1869. Suez Canal opened. Sainte-Beuve died. Blackmore: Lorna Doone. |
| 1870. Saint Paul and Protestantism. | 1870. War between France and Prussia; the third republic in France; Rome capital of the kingdom of Italy. Dickens died. Huxley: Lay Sermons. D. G. Rossetti: Poems. Bret Harte: Luck of Roaring Camp. |
| 1871. Friendship's Garland. | 1871. The German Empire; the Commune at Paris. Darwin: Descent of Man. G. Meredith: Harry Richmond. Swinburne: Songs before Sunrise. |
| 1873. Literature and Dogma. | 1873. J. S. Mill died. Pater: Studies in the Renaissance. |
| 1874. Higher Schools and Universities of Germany. | 1874. Disraeli prime minister. Hardy: Far from the Madding Crowd. Thomson: City of Dreadful Night. |
| 1875. God and the Bible. | |
| | 1876. George Sand died. W. Morris: Sigurd the Volsung. |
| 1877. Edited a volume of selections from his poems. Last Essays on Church and Religion. | 1877. Russo - Turkish War. Hardy: Return of the Native. Tennyson: Harold. Ibsen: Pillars of Society. Tolstoi: Anna Karénina. Turgenef: Virgin Soil. |
| 1878. Edited six of Johnson's Lives of the Poets. | |
| 1879. Mixed Essays Edited Selections from Wordsworth. | 1879. G. Meredith: The Egoist. Ibsen: A Doll's House. Zola: L'Assommoir. H. James: Daisy Miller. |
| | 1880. George Eliot and Flaubert died |

# CHRONOLOGICAL TABLE

| Arnold's Life and Works. | Contemporary Literature and History. |
|---|---|
| 1881. Edited Selections from Byron, and Selections from Burke. | 1881. Assassination of the Czar, Alexander II, and of President Garfield. Carlyle and Lord Beaconsfield (Disraeli) died. Carlyle: Reminiscences. D. G. Rossetti: Ballads and Sonnets. Stevenson: Virginibus puerisque. Swinburne: Mary Stuart. |
| 1882. Irish Essays. | 1882. Darwin, Rossetti, Trollope, Longfellow, and Emerson died. |
| 1883. Received a pension from the government. | 1883. British occupation of Egypt. Stevenson: Treasure Island. |
| 1883–4. Lectured in America. | 1884. Browning: Ferishtah's Fancies. Tennyson: Becket. Daudet: Sapho. Mark Twain: Huckleberry Finn. |
| 1885. Discourses in America. | 1885. Gladstone adopts Home Rule. Victor Hugo died. G. Meredith: Diana of the Crossways. Pater: Marius the Epicurean. Ruskin: Praeterita. Zola: Germinal. |
| 1886. Revisited America. Retired from the inspectorship of schools. | 1886. Home Rule Bill defeated. Stevenson: Kidnapped. Tennyson: Locksley Hall Sixty Years After, and other poems. |
| 1888. April 15, died. Essays in Criticism, second series. | |
| | 1889. Browning died. |
| | 1890. Bismarck dismissed from office. Newman died. |
| | 1892. Tennyson died. |

# SOHRAB AND RUSTUM
## AND OTHER POEMS

MATTHEW ARNOLD

# SOHRAB AND RUSTUM

### AN EPISODE

AND the first grey of morning fill'd the east,
And the fog rose out of the Oxus stream.
But all the Tartar camp along the stream
Was hush'd, and still the men were plunged in sleep;
Sohrab alone, he slept not; all night long   5
He had lain wakeful, tossing on his bed;
But when the grey dawn stole into his tent,
He rose, and clad himself, and girt his sword,
And took his horseman's cloak and left his tent,
And went abroad into the cold wet fog,   10
Through the dim camp to Peran-Wisa's tent.

Through the black Tartar tents he pass'd, which stood
Clustering like bee-hives on the low flat strand
Of Oxus, where the summer-floods o'erflow
When the sun melts the snows in high Pamere;   15
Through the black tents he pass'd, o'er that low strand,
And to a hillock came, a little back
From the stream's brink—the spot where first a boat,
Crossing the stream in summer, scrapes the land.
The men of former times had crown'd the top   20
With a clay fort; but that was fall'n, and now
The Tartars built there Peran-Wisa's tent,
A dome of laths, and o'er it felts were spread.
And Sohrab came there, and went in, and stood
Upon the thick piled carpets in the tent,   25

And found the old man sleeping on his bed
Of rugs and felts, and near him lay his arms.
And Peran-Wisa heard him, though the step
Was dull'd; for he slept light, an old man's sleep;
And he rose quickly on one arm, and said:— 30
 "Who art thou? for it is not yet clear dawn.
Speak! is there news, or any night alarm?"
 But Sohrab came to the bedside, and said:—
"Thou know'st me, Peran-Wisa! it is I.
The sun is not yet risen, and the foe 35
Sleep; but I sleep not; all night long I lie
Tossing and wakeful, and I come to thee.
For so did King Afrasiab bid me seek
Thy counsel, and to heed thee as thy son,
In Samarcand, before the army march'd; 40
And I will tell thee what my heart desires.
Thou know'st if, since from Ader-baijan first
I came among the Tartars and bore arms,
I have still served Afrasiab well, and shown,
At my boy's years, the courage of a man. 45
This too thou know'st, that while I still bear on
The conquering Tartar ensigns through the world,
And beat the Persians back on every field,
I seek one man, one man, and one alone—
Rustum, my father; who I hoped should greet, 50
Should one day greet, upon some well-fought field,
His not unworthy, not inglorious son.
So I long hoped, but him I never find.
Come then, hear now, and grant me what I ask.
Let the two armies rest to-day; but I 55
Will challenge forth the bravest Persian lords
To meet me, man to man; if I prevail,
Rustum will surely hear it; if I fall—

Old man, the dead need no one, claim no kin.
Dim is the rumour of a common fight,
Where host meets host, and many names are sunk;
But of a single combat fame speaks clear."

He spoke; and Peran-Wisa took the hand
Of the young man in his, and sigh'd, and said:—

"O Sohrab, an unquiet heart is thine!
Canst thou not rest among the Tartar chiefs,
And share the battle's common chance with us
Who love thee, but must press for ever first,
In single fight incurring single risk,
To find a father thou hast never seen?
That were far best, my son, to stay with us
Unmurmuring; in our tents, while it is war,
And when 'tis truce, then in Afrasiab's towns.
But, if this one desire indeed rules all,
To seek out Rustum—seek him not through fight!
Seek him in peace, and carry to his arms,
O Sohrab, carry an unwounded son!
But far hence seek him, for he is not here.
For now it is not as when I was young,
When Rustum was in front of every fray;
But now he keeps apart, and sits at home,
In Seistan, with Zal, his father old.
Whether that his own mighty strength at last
Feels the abhorr'd approaches of old age,
Or in some quarrel with the Persian King.
There go!—Thou wilt not? Yet my heart forebodes
Danger or death awaits thee on this field.
Fain would I know thee safe and well, though lost
To us; fain therefore send thee hence, in peace
To seek thy father, not seek single fights
In vain;—but who can keep the lion's cub

From ravening, and who govern Rustum's son?
Go, I will grant thee what thy heart desires."

So said he, and dropp'd Sohrab's hand, and left
His bed, and the warm rugs whereon he lay;  95
And o'er his chilly limbs his woollen coat
He pass'd, and tied his sandals on his feet,
And threw a white cloak round him, and he took
In his right hand a ruler's staff, no sword;
And on his head he set his sheep-skin cap,  100
Black, glossy, curl'd, the fleece of Kara-Kul;
And raised the curtain of his tent, and call'd
His herald to his side, and went abroad.

The sun by this had risen, and clear'd the fog
From the broad Oxus and the glittering sands  105
And from their tents the Tartar horsemen filed
Into the open plain; so Haman bade—
Haman, who next to Peran-Wisa ruled
The host, and still was in his lusty prime.
From their black tents, long files of horse, they stream'd;
As when some grey November morn the files,  111
In marching order spread, of long-neck'd cranes
Stream over Casbin and the southern slopes
Of Elburz, from the Aralian estuaries,
Or some frore Caspian reed-bed, southward bound  115
For the warm Persian sea-board—so they stream'd.
The Tartars of the Oxus, the King's guard,
First, with black sheep-skin caps and with long spears;
Large men, large steeds; who from Bokhara come
And Khiva, and ferment the milk of mares.  120
Next, the more temperate Toorkmuns of the south,
The Tukas, and the lances of Salore,
And those from Attruck and the Caspian sands;
Light men and on light steeds, who only drink

The acrid milk of camels, and their wells. 125
And then a swarm of wandering horse, who came
From far, and a more doubtful service own'd;
The Tartars of Ferghana, from the banks
Of the Jaxartes, men with scanty beards
And close-set skull-caps; and those wilder hordes 130
Who roam o'er Kipchak and the northern waste,
Kalmucks and unkempt Kuzzaks, tribes who stray
Nearest the Pole, and wandering Kirghizzes,
Who come on shaggy ponies from Pamere;
These all filed out from camp into the plain. 135
And on the other side the Persians form'd,—
First a light cloud of horse, Tartars they seem'd,
The Ilyats of Khorassan; and behind,
The royal troops of Persia, horse and foot,
Marshall'd battalions bright in burnish'd steel. 140
But Peran-Wisa with his herald came,
Threading the Tartar squadrons to the front,
And with his staff kept back the foremost ranks.
And when Ferood, who led the Persians, saw
That Peran-Wisa kept the Tartars back, 145
He took his spear, and to the front he came,
And check'd his ranks, and fix'd them where they stood.
And the old Tartar came upon the sand
Betwixt the silent hosts, and spake, and said:—

"Ferood, and ye, Persians and Tartars, hear! 150
Let there be truce between the hosts to-day.
But choose a champion from the Persian lords
To fight our champion Sohrab, man to man."

As, in the country, on a morn in June,
When the dew glistens on the pearled ears, 155
A shiver runs through the deep corn for joy—
So, when they heard what Peran-Wisa said,

A thrill through all the Tartar squadrons ran
Of pride and hope for Sohrab, whom they loved.

 But as a troop of pedlars, from Cabool,     160
Cross underneath the Indian Caucasus,
That vast sky-neighbouring mountain of milk snow;
Crossing so high, that, as they mount, they pass
Long flocks of travelling birds dead on the snow,
Choked by the air, and scarce can they themselves   165
Slake their parch'd throats with sugar'd mulberries—
In single file they move, and stop their breath,
For fear they should dislodge the o'erhanging snows—
So the pale Persians held their breath with fear.

 And to Ferood his brother chiefs came up     170
To counsel; Gudurz and Zoarrah came,
And Feraburz, who ruled the Persian host
Second, and was the uncle of the King;
These came and counsell'd, and then Gudurz said:—

 "Ferood, shame bids us take their challenge up,   175
Yet champion have we none to match this youth.
He has the wild stag's foot, the lion's heart.
But Rustum came last night; aloof he sits
And sullen, and has pitch'd his tents apart.
Him will I seek, and carry to his ear       180
The Tartar challenge, and this young man's name.
Haply he will forget his wrath, and fight.
Stand forth the while, and take their challenge up."

 So spake he; and Ferood stood forth and cried:—
"Old man, be it agreed as thou hast said!     185
Let Sohrab arm, and we will find a man."

 He spake: and Peran-Wisa turn'd, and strode
Back through the opening squadrons to his tent.
But through the anxious Persians Gudurz ran,
And cross'd the camp which lay behind, and reach'd,

Out on the sands beyond it, Rustum's tents. 191
Of scarlet cloth they were, and glittering gay,
Just pitch'd; the high pavilion in the midst
Was Rustum's, and his men lay camp'd around.
And Gudurz enter'd Rustum's tent, and found 195
Rustum; his morning meal was done, but still
The table stood before him, charged with food—
A side of roasted sheep, and cakes of bread,
And dark green melons; and there Rustum sate
Listless, and held a falcon on his wrist, 200
And play'd with it; but Gudurz came and stood
Before him; and he look'd, and saw him stand,
And with a cry sprang up and dropp'd the bird,
And greeted Gudurz with both hands, and said:—
  "Welcome! these eyes could see no better sight. 205
What news? but sit down first, and eat and drink."
  But Gudurz stood in the tent-door, and said:—
"Not now! a time will come to eat and drink,
But not to-day; to-day has other needs.
The armies are drawn out, and stand at gaze; 210
For from the Tartars is a challenge brought
To pick a champion from the Persian lords
To fight their champion—and thou know'st his name—
Sohrab men call him, but his birth is hid.
O Rustum, like thy might is this young man's! 215
He has the wild stag's foot, the lion's heart;
And he is young, and Iran's chiefs are old,
Or else too weak; and all eyes turn to thee.
Come down and help us, Rustum, or we lose!"
  He spoke; but Rustum answer'd with a smile:— 220
"Go to! if Iran's chiefs are old, then I
Am older; if the young are weak, the King
Errs strangely; for the King, for Kai Khosroo,

Himself is young, and honours younger men,
And lets the aged moulder to their graves. 225
Rustum he loves no more, but loves the young—
The young may rise at Sohrab's vaunts, not I.
For what care I, though all speak Sohrab's fame?
For would that I myself had such a son,
And not that one slight helpless girl I have— 230
A son so famed, so brave, to send to war,
And I to tarry with the snow-hair'd Zal,
My father, whom the robber Afghans vex,
And clip his borders short, and drive his herds,
And he has none to guard his weak old age. 235
There would I go, and hang my armour up,
And with my great name fence that weak old man,
And spend the goodly treasures I have got,
And rest my age, and hear of Sohrab's fame,
And leave to death the hosts of thankless kings, 240
And with these slaughterous hands draw sword no more."

He spoke, and smiled; and Gudurz made reply:—
"What then, O Rustum, will men say to this,
When Sohrab dares our bravest forth, and seeks
Thee most of all, and thou, whom most he seeks, 245
Hidest thy face? Take heed lest men should say:
*Like some old miser, Rustum hoards his fame,
And shuns to peril it with younger men.*"

And, greatly moved, then Rustum made reply:—
"O Gudurz, wherefore dost thou say such words? 250
Thou knowest better words than this to say.
What is one more, one less, obscure or famed,
Valiant or craven, young or old, to me?
Are not they mortal, am not I myself?
But who for men of nought would do great deeds? 255
Come, thou shalt see how Rustum hoards his fame.

But I will fight unknown, and in plain arms;
Let not men say of Rustum, he was match'd
In single fight with any mortal man."

  He spoke, and frown'd; and Gudurz turn'd, and ran
Back quickly through the camp in fear and joy—   261
Fear at his wrath, but joy that Rustum came.
But Rustum strode to his tent-door, and call'd
His followers in, and bade them bring his arms,
And clad himself in steel; the arms he chose   265
Were plain, and on his shield was no device,
Only his helm was rich, inlaid with gold,
And, from the fluted spine atop, a plume
Of horsehair waved, a scarlet horsehair plume.
So arm'd, he issued forth; and Ruksh, his horse,   270
Follow'd him like a faithful hound at heel—
Ruksh, whose renown was noised through all the earth,
The horse, whom Rustum on a foray once
Did in Bokhara by the river find
A colt beneath its dam, and drove him home,   275
And rear'd him; a bright bay, with lofty crest,
Dight with a saddle-cloth of broider'd green
Crusted with gold, and on the ground were work'd
All beasts of chase, all beasts which hunters know.
So follow'd, Rustum left his tents, and cross'd   280
The camp, and to the Persian host appear'd.
And all the Persians knew him, and with shouts
Hail'd; but the Tartars knew not who he was.
And dear as the wet diver to the eyes
Of his pale wife who waits and weeps on shore,   285
By sandy Bahrein, in the Persian Gulf,
Plunging all day in the blue waves, at night,
Having made up his tale of precious pearls,
Rejoins her in their hut upon the sands—

So dear to the pale Persians Rustum came. 290
  And Rustum to the Persian front advanced,
And Sohrab arm'd in Haman's tent, and came.
And as afield the reapers cut a swath
Down through the middle of a rich man's corn,
And on each side are squares of standing corn, 295
And in the midst a stubble, short and bare—
So on each side were squares of men, with spears
Bristling, and in the midst, the open sand.
And Rustum came upon the sand, and cast
His eyes toward the Tartar tents, and saw 300
Sohrab come forth, and eyed him as he came.

  As some rich woman, on a winter's morn,
Eyes through her silken curtains the poor drudge
Who with numb blacken'd fingers makes her fire—
At cock-crow, on a starlit winter's morn, 305
When the frost flowers the whiten'd window-panes—
And wonders how she lives, and what the thoughts
Of that poor drudge may be; so Rustum eyed
The unknown adventurous youth, who from afar
Came seeking Rustum, and defying forth 310
All the most valiant chiefs; long he perused
His spirited air, and wonder'd who he was.
For very young he seem'd, tenderly rear'd;
Like some young cypress, tall, and dark, and straight,
Which in a queen's secluded garden throws 315
Its slight dark shadow on the moonlit turf,
By midnight, to a bubbling fountain's sound—
So slender Sohrab seem'd, so softly rear'd.
And a deep pity enter'd Rustum's soul
As he beheld him coming; and he stood, 320
And beckon'd to him with his hand, and said:—

  "O thou young man, the air of Heaven is soft,

And warm, and pleasant; but the grave is cold!
Heaven's air is better than the cold dead grave.
Behold me! I am vast, and clad in iron, 325
And tried; and I have stood on many a field
Of blood, and I have fought with many a foe—
Never was that field lost, or that foe saved.
O Sohrab, wherefore wilt thou rush on death?
Be govern'd! quit the Tartar host, and come 330
To Iran, and be as my son to me,
And fight beneath my banner till I die!
There are no youths in Iran brave as thou."

So he spake, mildly; Sohrab heard his voice,
The mighty voice of Rustum, and he saw 335
His giant figure planted on the sand,
Sole, like some single tower, which a chief
Hath builded on the waste in former years
Against the robbers; and he saw that head,
Streak'd with its first grey hairs;—hope filled his soul,
And he ran forward and embraced his knees, 341
And clasp'd his hand within his own, and said:—

"O, by thy father's head! by thine own soul!
Art thou not Rustum? speak! art thou not he?"

But Rustum eyed askance the kneeling youth, 345
And turn'd away, and spake to his own soul:—

"Ah me, I muse what this young fox may mean!
False, wily, boastful, are these Tartar boys.
For if I now confess this thing he asks,
And hide it not, but say: *Rustum is here!* 350
He will not yield indeed, nor quit our foes,
But he will find some pretext not to fight.
And praise my fame, and proffer courteous gifts
A belt or sword perhaps, and go his way.
And on a feast-tide, in Afrasiab's hall, 355

In Samarcand, he will arise and cry:
"'I challenged once, when the two armies camp'd
Besides the Oxus, all the Persian lords
To cope with me in single fight; but they
Shrank, only Rustum dared; then he and I        360
Changed gifts, and went on equal terms away.'
So will he speak, perhaps, while men applaud;
Then were the chiefs of Iran shamed through me."

And then he turn'd, and sternly spake aloud:—
"Rise! wherefore dost thou vainly question thus      365
Of Rustum? I am here, whom thou hast call'd
By challenge forth; make good thy vaunt, or yield!
Is it with Rustum only thou wouldst fight?
Rash boy, men look on Rustum's face and flee!
For well I know that did great Rustum stand         370
Before thy face this day, and were reveal'd,
There would be then no talk of fighting more.
But being what I am, I tell thee this—
Do thou record it in thine inmost soul:
Either thou shalt renounce thy vaunt and yield,      375
Or else thy bones shall strew this sand, till winds
Bleach them, or Oxus with his summer-floods,
Oxus in summer wash them all away."

He spoke; and Sohrab answer'd, on his feet:—
"Art thou so fierce? Thou wilt not fright me so!    380
I am no girl, to be made pale by words.
Yet this thou hast said well, did Rustum stand
Here on this field, there were no fighting then.
But Rustum is far hence, and we stand here.
Begin! thou are more vast, more dread than I,        385
And thou art proved, I know, and I am young—
But yet success sways with the breath of Heaven.
And though thou thinkest that thou knowest sure

Thy victory, yet thou canst not surely know.
For we are all, like swimmers in the sea, 390
Poised on the top of a huge wave of fate,
Which hangs uncertain to which side to fall.
And whether it will heave us up to land,
Or whether it will roll us out to sea,
Back out to sea, to the deep waves of death, 395
We know not, and no search will make us know;
Only the event will teach us in its hour."

He spoke, and Rustum answer'd not, but hurl'd
His spear; down from the shoulder, down it came,
As on some partridge in the corn a hawk, 400
That long has tower'd in the airy clouds,
Drops like a plummet; Sohrab saw it come,
And sprang aside, quick as a flash; the spear
Hiss'd, and went quivering down into the sand,
Which it sent flying wide;—then Sohrab threw 405
In turn, and full struck Rustum's shield; sharp rang,
The iron plates rang sharp, but turn'd the spear.
And Rustum seized his club, which none but he
Could wield; an unlopp'd trunk it was, and huge,
Still rough—like those which men in treeless plains 410
To build them boats fish from the flooded rivers.
Hyphasis or Hydaspes, when, high up
By their dark springs, the wind in winter-time
Hath made in Himalayan forests wrack,
And strewn the channels with torn boughs—so huge 415
The club which Rustum lifted now, and struck
One stroke; but again Sohrab sprang aside,
Lithe as the glancing snake, and the club came
Thundering to earth, and leapt from Rustum's hand.
And Rustum follow'd his own blow, and fell 420
To his knees, and with his fingers clutch'd the sand;

And now might Sohrab have unsheathed his sword,
And pierced the mighty Rustum while he lay
Dizzy, and on his knees, and choked with sand;
But he look'd on, and smiled, nor bared his sword, 425
But courteously drew back and spoke, and said:—

"Thou strik'st too hard! that club of thine will float
Upon the summer-floods, and not my bones.
But rise, and be not wroth! not wroth am I;
No, when I see thee, wrath forsakes my soul. 430
Thou say'st, thou art not Rustum; be it so!
Who art thou then, that canst so touch my soul?
Boy as I am, I have seen battles too—
Have waded foremost in their bloody waves,
And heard their hollow roar of dying men; 435
But never was my heart thus touched before.
Are they from Heaven, these softenings of the heart?
O thou old warrior, let us yield to Heaven!
Come, plant we here in earth our angry spears,
And make a truce, and sit upon this sand, 440
And pledge each other in red wine, like friends,
And thou shalt talk to me of Rustum's deeds.
There are enough foes in the Persian host,
Whom I may meet, and strike, and feel no pang;
Champions enough Afrasiab has, whom thou 445
Mayst fight; fight *them*, when they confront thy spear!
But oh, let there be peace 'twixt thee and me!"

He ceased, but while he spake, Rustum had risen,
And stood erect, trembling with rage; his club
He left to lie, but had regain'd his spear, 450
Whose fiery point now in his mail'd right-hand
Blazed bright and baleful, like that autumn-star,
The baleful sign of fevers; dust had soil'd
His stately crest, and dimm'd his glittering arms. 454

His breast heaved, his lips foam'd, and twice his voice
Was choked with rage; at last these words broke way:—
  "Girl! nimble with thy feet, not with thy hands!
Curl'd minion, dancer, coiner of sweet words!
Fight, let me hear thy hateful voice no more!
Thou art not in Afrasiab's gardens now            460
With Tartar girls, with whom thou art wont to dance;
But on the Oxus-sands, and in the dance
Of battle, and with me, who make no play
Of war; I fight it out, and hand to hand.
Speak not to me of truce, and pledge, and wine!   465
Remember all thy valour; try thy feints
And cunning! all the pity I had is gone;
Because thou hast shamed me before both the hosts
With thy light skipping tricks, and thy girl's wiles."
  He spoke, and Sohrab kindled at his taunts,     470
And he too drew his sword; at once they rush'd
Together, as two eagles on one prey
Come rushing down together from the clouds,
One from the east, one from the west; their shields
Dash'd with a clang together, and a din          475
Rose, such as that the sinewy woodcutters
Make often in the forest's heart at morn,
Of hewing axes, crashing trees—such blows
Rustum and Sohrab on each other hail'd.
And you would say that sun and stars took part   480
In that unnatural conflict; for a cloud
Grew suddenly in Heaven, and dark'd the sun
Over the fighters' heads; and a wind rose
Under their feet, and moaning swept the plain,
And in a sandy whirlwind wrapp'd the pair.       485
In gloom they twain were wrapp'd, and they alone;
For both the on-looking hosts on either hand

Stood in broad daylight, and the sky was pure,
And the sun sparkled on the Oxus stream.
But in the gloom they fought, with bloodshot eyes   490
And labouring breath; first Rustum struck the shield
Which Sohrab held stiff out; the steel-piked spear
Rent the tough plates, but fail'd to reach the skin,
And Rustum pluck'd it back with angry groan.
Then Sohrab with his sword smote Rustum's helm,   495
Nor clove its steel quite through; but all the crest
He shore away, and that proud horsehair plume,
Never till now defiled, sank to the dust;
And Rustum bow'd his head; but then the gloom
Grew blacker, thunder rumbled in the air,   500
And lightnings rent the cloud; and Ruksh, the horse,
Who stood at hand, utter'd a dreadful cry;—
No horse's cry was that, most like the roar
Of some pain'd desert-lion, who all day
Hath trail'd the hunter's javelin in his side,   505
And comes at night to die upon the sand.
The two hosts heard that cry, and quaked for fear,
And Oxus curdled as it cross'd his stream.
But Sohrab heard, and quail'd not, but rush'd on,
And struck again; and again Rustum bow'd   510
His head; but this time all the blade, like glass,
Sprang in a thousand shivers on the helm,
And in the hand the hilt remain'd alone.
Then Rustum raised his head; his dreadful eyes
Glared, and he shook on high his menacing spear,   515
And shouted: *Rustum!*—Sohrab heard that shout,
And shrank amazed; back he recoil'd one step,
And scann'd with blinking eyes the advancing form;
And then he stood bewilder'd; and he dropp'd
His covering shield, and the spear pierced his side.   520

He reel'd, and staggering back, sank to the ground;
And then the gloom dispersed, and the wind fell,
And the bright sun broke forth, and melted all
The cloud; and the two armies saw the pair—
Saw Rustum standing, safe upon his feet, 525
And Sohrab, wounded, on the bloody sand.

Then, with a bitter smile, Rustum began:—
"Sohrab, thou thoughtest in thy mind to kill
A Persian lord this day, and strip his corpse,
And bear thy trophies to Afrasiab's tent. 530
Or else that the great Rustum would come down
Himself to fight, and that thy wiles would move
His heart to take a gift, and let thee go.
And then that all the Tartar host would praise
Thy courage or thy craft, and spread thy fame, 535
To glad thy father in his weak old age.
Fool, thou art slain, and by an unknown man!
Dearer to the red jackals shalt thou be
Than to thy friends, and to thy father old."

And, with a fearless mien, Sohrab replied:— 540
"Unknown thou art; yet thy fierce vaunt is vain.
Thou dost not slay me, proud and boastful man!
No! Rustum slays me, and this filial heart.
For were I match'd with ten such man as thee,
And I were that which till to-day I was, 545
They should be lying here, I standing there.
But that belovéd name unnerved my arm—
That name, and something, I confess, in thee,
Which troubles all my heart, and made my shield
Fall; and thy spear transfix'd an unarm'd foe. 550
And now thou boastest, and insult'st my fate.
But hear thou this, fierce man, tremble to hear:
The mighty Rustum shall avenge my death!

My father, whom I seek through all the world,
He shall avenge my death, and punish thee!'"     555
  As when some hunter in the spring hath found
A breeding eagle sitting on her nest,
Upon the craggy isle of a hill-lake,
And pierced her with an arrow as she rose,
And follow'd her to find her where she fell     560
Far off;—anon her mate comes winging back
From hunting, and a great way off descries
His huddling young left sole; at that, he checks
His pinion, and with short uneasy sweeps
Circles above his eyry, with loud screams     565
Chiding his mate back to her nest; but she
Lies dying, with the arrow in her side,
In some far stony gorge out of his ken,
A heap of fluttering feathers—never more
Shall the lake glass her, flying over it;     570
Never the black and dripping precipices
Echo her stormy scream as she sails by—
As that poor bird flies home, nor knows his loss,
So Rustum knew not his own loss, but stood
Over his dying son, and knew him not.     575
  But, with a cold incredulous voice, he said:—
"What prate is this of fathers and revenge?
The mighty Rustum never had a son."
  And, with a failing voice, Sohrab replied:—
"Ah yes, he had! and that lost son am I.     580
Surely the news will one day reach his ear,
Reach Rustum, where he sits, and tarries long,
Somewhere, I know not where, but far from here;
And pierce him like a stab, and make him leap
To arms, and cry for vengeance upon thee.     585
Fierce man, bethink thee, for an only son!

What will that grief, what will that vengeance be?
Oh, could I live, till I that grief had seen!
Yet him I pity not so much, but her,
My mother, who in Ader-baijan dwells               590
With that old king, her father, who grows grey
With age, and rules over the valiant Koords.
Her most I pity, who no more will see
Sohrab returning from the Tartar camp,
With spoils and honour, when the war is done.     595
But a dark rumour will be bruited up,
From tribe to tribe, until it reach her ear;
And then will that defenceless woman learn
That Sohrab will rejoice her sight no more,
But that in battle with a nameless foe,           600
By the far-distant Oxus, he is slain."

  He spoke; and as he ceased, he wept aloud,
Thinking of her he left, and his own death.
He spoke; but Rustum listen'd, plunged in thought.
Nor did he yet believe it was his son              605
Who spoke, although he call'd back names he knew;
For he had had sure tidings that the babe,
Which was in Ader-baijan born to him,
Had been a puny girl, no boy at all—
So that sad mother sent him word, for fear        610
Rustum should seek the boy, to train in arms—
And so he deem'd that either Sohrab took,
By a false boast, the style of Rustum's son;
Or that men gave it him, to swell his fame.
So deem'd he; yet he listen'd, plunged in thought, 615
And his soul set to grief, as the vast tide
Of the bright rocking Ocean sets to shore
At the full moon; tears gather'd in his eyes;
For he remember'd his own early youth

And all its bounding rapture; as, at dawn, 620
The shepherd from his mountain-lodge descries
A far, bright city, smitten by the sun,
Through many rolling clouds—so Rustum saw
His youth; saw Sohrab's mother, in her bloom;
And that old king, her father, who loved well 625
His wandering guest, and gave him his fair child
With joy; and all the pleasant life they led,
They three, in that long-distant summer-time—
The castle, and the dewy woods, and hunt
And hound, and morn on those delightful hills 630
In Ader-baijan. And he saw that Youth,
Of age and looks to be his own dear son,
Piteous and lovely, lying on the sand,
Like some rich hyacinth which by the scythe
Of an unskilful gardener has been cut, 635
Mowing the garden grass-plots near its bed,
And lies, a fragrant tower of purple bloom,
On the mown, dying grass—so Sohrab lay,
Lovely in death, upon the common sand.
And Rustum gazed on him with grief, and said:— 640
  "O Sohrab, thou indeed art such a son
Whom Rustum, wert thou his, might well have loved.
Yet here thou errest, Sohrab, or else men
Have told thee false—thou art not Rustum's son.
For Rustum had no son; one child he had— 645
But one—a girl; who with her mother now
Plies some light female task, nor dreams of us—
Of us she dreams not, nor of wounds, nor war."
  But Sohrab answer'd him in wrath; for now
The anguish of the deep-fix'd spear grew fierce, 650
And he desired to draw forth the steel,
And let the blood flow free, and so to die—

But first he would convince his stubborn foe;
And, rising sternly on one arm, he said:—

"Man, who art thou who dost deny my words?  655
Truth sits u on the lips of dying men,
And falsehood, while I lived, was far from mine.
I tell thee, prick'd upon this arm I bear
That seal which Rustum to my mother gave,
That she might prick it on the babe she bore."  660

He spoke; and all the blood left Rustum's cheeks,
And his knees totter'd, and he smote his hand
Against his breast, his heavy mailed hand,
That the hard iron corslet clank'd aloud;
And to his heart he press'd the other hand,  665
And in a hollow voice he spake, and said:—

"Sohrab, that were a proof which could not lie!
If thou show this, then art thou Rustum's son."

Then, with weak hasty fingers, Sohrab loosed
His belt, and near the shoulder bared his arm,  670
And show'd a sign in faint vermilion points
Prick'd; as a cunning workman, in Pekin,
Pricks with vermilion some clear porcelain vase,
An emperor's gift—at early morn he paints,
And all day long, and, when night comes, the lamp  675
Lights up his studious forehead and thin hands—
So delicately prick'd the sign appear'd
On Sohrab's arm, the sign of Rustum's seal.
It was that griffin, which of old rear'd Zal,
Rustum's great father, whom they left to die,  680
A helpless babe, among the mountain-rocks;
Him that kind creature found, and rear'd, and loved—
Then Rustum took it for his glorious sign.
And Sohrab bared that image on his arm,
And himself scann'd it long with mournful eyes,  685

And then he touched it with his hand and said:—
"How say'st thou? Is that sign the proper sign
Of Rustum's son, or of some other man's?"

He spoke; but Rustum gazed, and gazed, and stood
Speechless; and then he utter'd one sharp cry: 690
*boy—thy father!*—and his voice choked there.
And then a dark cloud pass'd before his eyes,
And his head swam, and he sank down to earth.
But Sohrab crawl'd to where he lay, and cast
His arms about his neck, and kiss'd his lips, 695
And with fond faltering fingers stroked his cheeks,
Trying to call him back to life; and life
Came back to Rustum, and he oped his eyes,
And they stood wide with horror; and he seized
In both his hands the dust which lay around, 700
And threw it on his head, and smirch'd his hair,—
His hair, and face, and beard, and glittering arms;
And strong convulsive groanings shook his breast,
And his sobs choked him; and he clutch'd his sword,
To draw it, and for ever let life out. 705
But Sohrab saw his thought, and held his hands,
And with a soothing voice, he spake, and said:—

"Father, forbear! for I but meet to-day
The doom which at my birth was written down
In Heaven, and thou art Heaven's unconscious hand. 710
Surely my heart cried out that it was thou,
When first I saw thee; and thy heart spoke too,
I know it! but fate trod those promptings down
Under its iron heel; fate, fate engaged
The strife, and hurl'd me on my father's spear. 715
But let us speak no more of this! I find
My father; let me feel that I have found!
Come, sit beside me on this sand, and take

My head betwixt thy hands, and kiss my cheeks,
And wash them with thy tears, and say: *My son!*  720
Quick! quick! for number'd are my sands of life,
And swift; for like the lightning to this field
I came, and like the wind I go away—
Sudden, and swift, and like a passing wind.
But it was writ in Heaven that this should be."  725

So said he, and his voice released the heart
Of Rustum, and his tears broke forth; he cast
His arms round his son's neck, and wept aloud,
And kiss'd him. And awe fell on both the hosts,
When they saw Rustum's grief; and Ruksh, the horse,
With his head bowing to the ground and mane  731
Sweeping the dust, came near, and in mute woe
First to the one then to the other moved
His head, as if inquiring what their grief
Might mean; and from his dark, compassionate eyes,  735
The big warm tears roll'd down, and caked the sand.
But Rustum chid him with stern voice, and said:—

"Ruksh, now thou grievest; but, O Ruksh, thy feet
Should first have rotted on their nimble joints,
Or ere they brought thy master to this field!"  740

But Sohrab look'd upon the horse and said;—
"Is this, then, Ruksh? How often, in past days,
My mother told me of thee, thou brave steed,
My terrible father's terrible horse! and said,
That I should one day find thy lord and thee.
Come, let me lay my hand upon thy mane!  745
O Ruksh, thou are more fortunate than I;
For thou hast gone where I shall never go,
And snuff'd the breezes of my father's home.
And thou hast trod the sands of Seistan,  750
And seen the River of Helmund, and the Lake

Of Zirrah; and the aged Zal himself
Has often stroked thy neck, and given thee food,
Corn in a golden platter soak'd with wine,
And said; *O Ruksh! bear Rustum well!*—but I 755
Have never known my grandsire's furrow'd face,
Nor seen his lofty house in Seistan,
Nor slaked my thirst at the clear Helmund stream;
But lodged among my father's foes, and seen
Afrasiab's cities only, Samarcand, 760
Bokhara, and lone Khiva in the waste,
And the black Toorkmun tents; and only drunk
The desert rivers, Moorghab and Tejend,
Kohik, and where the Kalmuks feed their sheep,
The northern Sir; and this great Oxus stream, 765
The yellow Oxus, by whose brink I die."

Then, with a heavy groan, Rustum bewail'd:—
"Oh, that its waves were flowing over me!
Oh, that I saw its grains of yellow silt
Roll tumbling in the current o'er my head!" 770

But, with a grave mild voice, Sohrab replied:—
"Desire not that, my father! thou must live.
For some are born to do great deeds, and live,
As some are born to be obscured, and die.
Do thou the deeds I die too young to do, 775
And reap a second glory in thine age;
Thou art my father, and thy gain is mine.
But come! thou seest this great host of men
Which follow me; I pray thee, slay not these!
Let me entreat for them; what have they done? 780
They follow'd me, my hope, my fame, my star.
Let them all cross the Oxus back in peace.
But me thou must bear hence, not send with them,
But carry me with thee to Seistan,

And place me on a bed, and mourn for me, 785
Thou, and the snow-hair'd Zal, and all thy friends.
And thou must lay me in that lovely earth,
And heap a stately mound above my bones,
And plant a far-seen pillar over all.
That so the passing horseman on the waste 790
May see my tomb a great way off, and cry:
*Sohrab, the mighty Rustum's son, lies there,*
*Whom his great father did in ignorance kill!*
And I be not forgotten in my grave."

And, with a mournful voice, Rustum replied:— 795
"Fear not! as thou hast said, Sohrab, my son,
So shall it be; for I will burn my tents,
And quit the host, and bear thee hence with me,
And carry thee away to Seistan,
And place thee on a bed, and mourn for thee, 800
With the snow-headed Zal, and all my friends.
And I will lay thee in that lovely earth,
And heap a stately mound above thy bones,
And plant a far-seen pillar over all,
And men shall not forget thee in thy grave. 805
And I will spare thy host; yea, let them go!
Let them all cross the Oxus back in peace!
What should I do with slaying any more?
For would that all that I have ever slain
Might be once more alive; my bitterest foes, 810
And they who were call'd champions in their time,
And through whose death I won that fame I have—
And I were nothing but a common man,
A poor, mean soldier, and without renown,
So thou mightest live too, my son, my son! 815
Or rather would that I, even I myself,
Might now be lying on this bloody sand,

Near death, and by an ignorant stroke of thine,
Not thou of mine! and I might die, not thou;
And I, not thou, be borne to Seistan; 820
And Zal might weep above my grave, not thine;
And say: *O son, I weep thee not too sore,*
*For willingly, I know, thou met'st thine end!*
But now in blood and battles was my youth,
And full of blood and battles is my age, 825
And I shall never end this life of blood."

Then, at the point of death, Sohrab replied:—
"A life of blood indeed, thou dreadful man!
But thou shalt yet have peace; only not now,
Not yet! but thou shalt have it on that day, 830
When thou shalt sail in a high-masted ship,
Thou and the other peers of Kai Khosroo,
Returning home over the salt blue sea,
From laying thy dear master in his grave."

And Rustum gazed in Sohrab's face, and said:— 835
"Soon be that day, my son, and deep that sea!
Till then, if fate so wills, let me endure."

He spoke; and Sohrab smiled on him, and took
The spear, and drew it from his side, and eased
His wound's imperious anguish; but the blood 840
Came welling from the open gash, and life
Flow'd with the stream;—all down his cold white side
The crimson torrent ran, dim now and soil'd,
Like the soil'd tissue of white violets
Left, freshly gather'd, on their native bank, 845
By children whom their nurses call with haste
Indoors from the sun's eye; his head droop'd low,
His limbs grew slack; motionless, white, he lay—
White, with eyes closed; only when heavy gasps,
Deep heavy gasps quivering through all his frame, 850

Convulsed him back to life, he open'd them,
And fix'd them feebly on his father's face;
Till now all strength was ebb'd, and from his limbs
Unwillingly the spirit fled away,
Regretting the warm mansion which it left,  855
And youth, and bloom, and this delightful world.

So, on the bloody sand, Sohrab lay dead;
And the great Rustum drew his horseman's cloak
Down o'er his face, and sate by his dead son.
As those black granite pillars, once high-rear'd  860
By Jemshid in Persepolis, to bear
His house, now 'mid their broken flights of steps
Lie prone, enormous, down the mountain side—
So in the sand lay Rustum by his son.

And night came down over the solemn waste,  865
And the two gazing hosts, and that sole pair,
And darken'd all; and a cold fog, with night,
Crept from the Oxus. Soon a hum arose,
As of a great assembly loosed, and fires
Began to twinkle through the fog; for now  870
Both armies moved to camp, and took their meal;
The Persians took it on the open sands
Southward, the Tartars by the river marge;
And Rustum and his son were left alone.

But the majestic river floated on,  875
Out of the mist and hum of that low land,
Into the frosty starlight, and there moved,
Rejoicing, through the hush'd Chorasmian waste,
Under the solitary moon;—he flow'd
Right for the polar star, past Orgunjè,  880
Brimming, and bright, and large; then sands begin
To hem his watery march, and dam his streams,
And split his currents: that for many a league

The shorn and parcell'd Oxus strains along
Through beds of sand and matted rushy isles— 885
Oxus, forgetting the bright speed he had
In his high mountain-cradle in Pamere,
A foil'd circuitous wanderer—till at last
The long'd-for dash of waves is heard, and wide
His luminous home of waters opens, bright 890
And tranquil, from whose floor the new-bathed stars
Emerge, and shine upon the Aral Sea.

# SELECTED POEMS

## QUIET WORK

ONE lesson, Nature, let me learn of thee,
One lesson which in every wind is blown,
One lesson of two duties kept at one
Though the loud world proclaim their enmity—

Of toil unsever'd from tranquillity  5
Of labour, that in lasting fruit outgrows
Far noisier schemes, accomplish'd in repose,
Too great for haste, too high for rivalry!

Yes, while on earth a thousand discords ring,
Man's fitful uproar mingling with his toil,  10
Still do thy sleepless ministers move on,

Their glorious tasks in silence perfecting;
Still working, blaming still our vain turmoil,
Labourers that shall not fail, when man is gone.

## SHAKESPEARE

OTHERS abide our question. Thou art free.
We ask and ask—Thou smilest and art still,
Out-topping knowledge. For the loftiest hill,
Who to the stars uncrowns his majesty,

Planting his steadfast footsteps in the sea,  5
Making the heaven of heavens his dwelling-place,

Spares but the cloudy border of his base
To the foil'd searching of mortality;

And thou, who didst the stars and sunbeams know,
Self-school'd, self-scann'd, self-honour'd, self-secure,   10
Didst tread on earth unguess'd at.—Better so!

All pains the immortal spirit must endure,
All weakness which impairs, all griefs which bow,
Find their sole speech in that victorious brow.


## REQUIESCAT

STREW on her roses, roses,
   And never a spray of yew
In quiet she reposes;
   Ah, would that I did too!

Her mirth the world required;   5
   She bathed it in smiles of glee
But her heart was tired, tired,
   And now they let her be.

Her life was turning, turning,
   In mazes of heat and sound.   10
But for peace her soul was yearning,
   And now peace laps her round.

Her cabin'd, ample spirit,
   It flutter'd and fail'd for breath.
To-night it doth inherit   15
   The vasty hall of death.

## THE FORSAKEN MERMAN

COME, dear children, let us away;
Down and away below!
Now my brothers call from the bay,
Now the great winds shoreward blow,
Now the salt tides seaward flow;  5
Now the wild white horses play,
Champ and chafe and toss in the spray.
Children dear, let us away!
This way, this way!

Call her once before you go—  10
Call once yet!
In a voice that she will know:
"Margaret! Margaret!"
Children's voices should be dear
(Call once more) to a mother's ear;  15
Children's voices, wild with pain—
Surely she will come again!
Call her once and come away;
This way, this way!
"Mother dear, we cannot stay!
The wild white horses foam and fret."  20
Margaret! Margaret!

Come, dear children, come away down;
Call no more!
One last look at the white-wall'd town,  25
And the little grey church on the windy shore;
Then come down!
She will not come though you call all day;
Come away, come away!

Children dear, was it yesterday 30
We heard the sweet bells over the bay?
In the caverns where we lay,
Through the surf and through the swell,
The far-off sound of a silver bell?
Sand-strewn caverns, cool and deep, 35
Where the winds are all asleep;
Where the spent lights quiver and gleam,
Where the salt weed sways in the stream,
Where the sea-beasts, ranged all round,
Feed in the ooze of their pasture-ground; 40
Where the sea-snakes coil and twine,
Dry their mail and bask in the brine;
Where great whales come sailing by,
Sail and sail, with unshut eye,
Round the world for ever and aye? 45
When did music come this way?
Children dear, was it yesterday?

Children dear, was it yesterday
(Call yet once) that she went away?
Once she sate with you and me, 50
On a red gold throne in the heart of the sea,
And the youngest sate on her knee.
She comb'd its bright hair, and she tended it well,
When down swung the sound of a far-off bell.
She sigh'd, she look'd up through the clear green sea; 55
She said: "I must go, for my kinsfolk pray
In the little grey church on the shore to-day.
'Twill be Easter-time in the world—ah me!
And I lose my poor soul, Merman! here with thee."
I said: "Go up, dear heart, through the waves; 60
Say thy prayer, and come back to the kind sea-caves!"

She smiled, she went up through the surf in the bay.
Children dear, was it yesterday?

  Children dear, were we long alone?
"The sea grows stormy, the little ones moan;     65
Long prayers," I said, "in the world they say;
Come!" I said; and we rose through the surf in the bay.
We went up the beach, by the sandy down
Where the sea-stocks bloom, to the white-wall'd town;
Through the narrow paved streets, where all was still,   70
To the little grey church on the windy hill.
From the church came a murmur of folk at their prayers,
But we stood without in the cold blowing airs.
We climb'd on the graves, on the stones worn with rains,
And we gazed up the aisle through the small leaded panes.
She sate by the pillar; we saw her clear:     76
"Margaret, hist! come quick, we are here!
Dear heart," I said, "we are long alone;
The sea grows stormy, the little ones moan."
But, ah, she gave me never a look,     80
For her eyes were seal'd to the holy book!
Loud prays the priest; shut stands the door.
Come away, children, call no more!
Come away, come down, call no more!

  Down, down, down!     85
Down to the depths of the sea!
She sits at her wheel in the humming town,
Singing most joyfully.
Hark what she sings: "O joy, O joy,
For the humming street, and the child with its toy!   90
For the priest, and the bell, and the holy well;
For the wheel where I spun,
And the blessed light of the sun!"

And so she sings her fill,
Singing most joyfully, 95
Till the spindle drops from her hand,
And the whizzing wheel stands still.
She steals to the window, and looks at the sand,
And over the sand at the sea;
And her eyes are set in a stare; 100
And anon there breaks a sigh,
And anon there drops a tear,
From a sorrow-clouded eye,
And a heart sorrow-laden,
A long, long sigh; 105
For the cold strange eyes of a little Mermaiden
And the gleam of her golden hair.

  Come away, away children;
Come children, come down!
The hoarse wind blows coldly; 110
Lights shine in the town.
She will start from her slumber
When gusts shake the door;
She will hear the winds howling,
Will hear the waves roar.
We shall see, while above us 115
The waves roar and whirl,
A ceiling of amber,
A pavement of pearl.
Singing: "Here came a mortal, 120
But faithless was she!
And alone dwell for ever
The kings of the sea."

But, children, at midnight,
When soft the winds blow, 125

When clear falls the moonlight,
When spring-tides are low;
When sweet airs come seaward
From heaths starr'd with broom,
And high rocks throw mildly 130
On the blanch'd sands a gloom;
Up the still, glistening beaches,
Up the creeks we will hie,
Over banks of bright seaweed
The ebb-tide leaves dry. 135
We will gaze, from the sand-hills,
At the white, sleeping town;
At the church on the hill-side—
And then come back down.
Singing: "There dwells a loved one, 140
But cruel is she!
She left lonely for ever
The kings of the sea."


## SWITZERLAND

#### MEETING

AGAIN I see my bliss at hand,
The town, the lake are here;
My Marguerite smiles upon the strand,
Unalter'd with the year.

I know that graceful figure fair, 5
That cheek of languid hue;
I know that soft, enkerchief'd hair,
And those sweet eyes of blue.

Again I spring to make my choice;
Again in tones of ire
I hear a God's tremendous voice:
"Be counsell'd, and retire."

Ye guiding Powers who join and part,
What would ye have with me?
Ah, warn some more ambitious heart,
And let the peaceful be!

### ISOLATION. TO MARGUERITE

We were apart; yet, day by day,
I bade my heart more constant be.
I bade it keep the world away,
And grow a home for only thee;
Nor fear'd but thy love likewise grew,
Like mine, each day, more tried, more true.

The fault was grave! I might have known,
What far too soon, alas! I learn'd—
The heart can bind itself alone,
And faith may oft be unreturn'd.
Self-sway'd our feelings ebb and swell—
Thou lov'st no more;—Farewell! Farewell!

Farewell!—and thou, thou lonely heart,
Which never yet without remorse
Even for a moment didst depart
From thy remote and spheréd course
To haunt the place where passions reign—
Back to thy solitude again!

Back! with the conscious thrill of shame
Which Luna felt, that summer-night, 20
Flash through her pure immortal frame,
When she forsook the starry height
To hang over Endymion's sleep
Upon the pine-grown Latmian steep.

Yet she, chaste queen, had never proved 25
How vain a thing is mortal love,
Wandering in Heaven, far removed.
But thou hast long had place to prove
This truth—to prove, and make thine own:
"Thou hast been, shalt be, art, alone." 30

Or, if not quite alone, yet they
Which touch thee are unmating things—
Ocean and clouds and night and day;
Lorn autumns and triumphant springs;
And life, and others' joy and pain, 35
And love, if love, of happier men.

Of happier men—for they, at least,
Have *dreamed* two human hearts might blend
In one, and were through faith released
From isolation without end 40
Prolong'd; nor knew, although not less
Alone than thou, their loneliness.

#### TO MARGUERITE—CONTINUED

Yes! in the sea of life enisled,
With echoing straits between us thrown,
Dotting the shoreless watery wild,

We mortal millions live *alone*.
The islands feel the enclasping flow,  5
And then their endless bounds they know.

But when the moon their hollows lights,
And they are swept by balms of spring,
And in their glens, on starry nights,
The nightingales divinely sing;  10
And lovely notes from shore to shore,
Across the sounds and channels pour—

Oh! then a longing like despair
Is to their farthest caverns sent;
For surely once, they feel, we were  15
Parts of a single continent!
Now round us spreads the watery plain—
Oh might our marges meet again!

Who order'd, that their longing's fire
Should be, as soon as kindled, cool'd?  20
Who renders vain their deep desire?—
A God, a God their severance ruled!
And bade betwixt their shores to be
The unplumb'd, salt, estranging sea.


## PHILOMELA

HARK! ah, the nightingale—
The tawny-throated!
Hark, from that moonlit cedar what a burst!
What triumph! hark!—what pain!

O wanderer from a Grecian shore,  25
Still, after many years, in distant lands,

Still nourishing in thy bewilder'd brain
That wild, unquench'd, deep-sunken, old-world pain—
Say, will it never heal?
And can this fragrant lawn
With its cool trees, and night,
And the sweet, tranquil Thames,
And moonshine, and the dew,
To thy rack'd heart and brain
Afford no balm?

Dost thou to-night behold,
Here, through the moonlight on this English grass,
The unfriendly palace in the Thracian wild?
Dost thou again peruse
With hot cheeks and sear'd eyes
The too clear web, and thy dumb sister's shame?
Dost thou once more assay
Thy flight, and feel come over thee,
Poor fugitive, the feathery change
Once more, and once more seem to make resound
With love and hate, triumph and agony,
Lone Daulis, and the high Cephissian vale?
Listen, Eugenia—
How thick the bursts come crowding through the leaves!
Again—thou hearest?
Eternal passion!
Eternal pain!

## DOVER BEACH

THE sea is calm to-night.
The tide is full, the moon lies fair
Upon the straits;—on the French coast the light
Gleams and is gone; the cliffs of England stand,
Glimmering and vast, out in the tranquil bay.  5
Come to the window, sweet is the night-air!
Only, from the long line of spray
Where the sea meets the moon-blanch'd land,
Listen! you hear the grating roar
Of pebbles which the waves draw back, and fling,  10
At their return, up the high strand,
Begin, and cease, and then again begin,
With tremulous cadence slow, and bring
The eternal note of sadness in.

Sophocles long ago  15
Heard it on the Ægæan, and it brought
Into his mind the turbid ebb and flow
Of human misery; we
Find also in the sound a thought,
Hearing it by this distant northern sea.  20

The Sea of Faith
Was once, too, at the full, and round earth's shore
Lay like the folds of a bright girdle furl'd.
But now I only hear
Its melancholy, long, withdrawing roar,  25
Retreating, to the breath
Of the night-wind, down the vast edges drear
And naked shingles of the world.

Ah, love, let us be true
To one another! for the world, which seems  30

To lie before us like a land of dreams,
So various, so beautiful, so new,
Hath really neither joy, nor love, nor light,
Nor certitude, nor peace, nor help for pain;
And we are here as on a darkling plain 35
Swept with confused alarms of struggle and flight,
Where ignorant armies clash by night.


BACCHANALIA;

OR, THE NEW AGE

I

THE evening comes, the fields are still.
The tinkle of the thirsty rill,
Unheard all day, ascends again;
Deserted is the half-mown plain,
Silent the swaths! the ringing wain, 5
The mower's cry, the dog's alarms,
All housed within the sleeping farms!
The business of the day is done,
The last-left haymaker is gone.
And from the thyme upon the height, 10
And from the elder-blossom white
And pale dog-roses in the hedge,
And from the mint-plant in the sedge,
In puffs of balm the night-air blows
The perfume which the day forgoes. 15
And on the pure horizon far,
See, pulsing with the first-born star,
The liquid sky above the hill!
The evening comes, the fields are still.

Loitering and leaping, 20
With saunter, with bounds—
Flickering and circling
In files and in rounds—
Gaily their pine-staff green
Tossing in air, 25
Loose o'er their shoulders white
Showering their hair—
See! the wild Mænads
Break from the wood,
Youth and Iacchus 30
Maddening their blood.
See! through the quiet land
Rioting they pass—
Fling the fresh heaps about,
Trample the grass. 35
Tear from the rifled hedge
Garlands, their prize;
Fill with their sports the field,
Fill with their cries.

   Shepherd, what ails thee, then? 40
Shepherd, why mute?
Forth with thy joyous song!
Forth with thy flute!
Tempts not the revel blithe?
Lure not their cries? 45
Glow not their shoulders smooth?
Melt not their eyes?
Is not, on cheeks like those,
Lovely the flush?
—*Ah, so the quiet was!* 50
*So was the hush!*

## II

The epoch ends, the world is still.
The age has talk'd and work'd its fill—
The famous orators have shone,
The famous poets sung and gone,
The famous men of war have fought,
The famous speculators thought,
The famous players, sculptors, wrought,
The famous painters fill'd their wall,
The famous critics judged it all.
The combatants are parted now—
Uphung the spear, unbent the bow,
The puissant crown'd, the weak laid low.
And in the after-silence sweet,
Now strifes are hush'd, our ears doth meet,
Ascending pure, the bell-like fame
Of this or that down-trodden name,
Delicate spirits, push'd away
In the hot press of the noon-day.
And o'er the plain, where the dead age
Did its now silent warfare wage—
O'er that wide plain now wrapt in gloom,
Where many a splendour finds its tomb,
Many spent fames and fallen mights—
The one or two immortal lights
Rise slowly up into the sky
To shine there everlastingly,
Like stars over the bounding hill.
The epoch ends, the world is still.

    Thundering and bursting
    In torrents, in waves—
    Carolling and shouting

Over tombs, amid graves—
See! on the cumber'd plain
Clearing a stage, 85
Scattering the past about,
Comes the new age.
Bards make new poems,
Thinkers new schools,
Statesmen new systems, 90
Critics new rules.
All things begin again;
Life is their prize;
Earth with their deeds they fill,
Fill with their cries. 95

Poet, what ails thee, then?
Say, why so mute?
Forth with thy praising voice!
Forth with thy flute!
Loiterer! why sittest thou 100
Sunk in thy dream?
Tempts not the bright new age?
Shines not its stream?
Look, ah, what genius,
Art, science, wit! 105
Soldiers like Cæsar
Statesmen like Pitt!
Sculptors like Phidias,
Raphaels in shoals,
Poets like Shakespeare— 110
Beautiful souls!
See, on their glowing cheeks
Heavenly the flush!
*—Ah, so the silence was!*
*So was the hush!* 115

The world but feels the present's spell,
The poet feels the past as well;
Whatever men have done, might do,
Whatever thought, might think it too.


## SELF-DEPENDENCE

WEARY of myself, and sick of asking
What I am, and what I ought to be,
At this vessel's prow I stand, which bears me
Forwards, forwards, o'er the starlit sea.

And a look of passionate desire
O'er the sea and to the stars I send:
"Ye who from my childhood up have calm'd me,
Calm me, ah, compose me to the end!

"Ah, once more," I cried, "ye stars, ye waters,
On my heart your mighty charm renew;
Still, still let me, as I gaze upon you,
Feel my soul becoming vast like you!"

From the intense, clear, star-sown vault of heaven,
Over the lit sea's unquiet way,
In the rustling night-air came the answer:
"Wouldst thou *be* as these are? *Live* as they.

"Unaffrighted by the silence round them,
Undistracted by the sights they see,
These demand not that the things without them
Yield them love, amusement, sympathy.

"And with joy the stars perform their shining,
And the sea its long moon-silver'd roll;
For self-poised they live, nor pine with noting
All the fever of some differing soul.

"Bounded by themselves, and unregardful  25
In what state God's other works may be,
In their own tasks all their powers pouring,
These attain the mighty life you see."

O air-born voice! long since, severely clear,
A cry like thine in mine own heart I hear:  30
"Resolve to be thyself; and know that he,
Who finds himself, loses his misery!"


## A SUMMER NIGHT

In the deserted, moon-blanch'd street,
How lonely rings the echo of my feet!
Those windows, which I gaze at, frown,
Silent and white, unopening down,
Repellent as the world;—but see,  5
A break between the housetops shows
The moon! and, lost behind her, fading dim
Into the dewy dark obscurity
Down at the far horizon's rim,
Doth a whole tract of heaven disclose!  10

And to my mind the thought
Is on a sudden brought
Of a past night, and a far different scene.
Headlands stood out into the moonlit deep
As clearly as at noon;  15

The spring-tide's brimming flow
Heaved dazzlingly between;
Houses, with long white sweep,
Girdled the glistening bay;
Behind, through the soft air,
The blue haze-cradled mountains spread away,
The night was far more fair—
But the same restless pacings to and fro,
And the same vainly throbbing heart was there,
And the same bright calm moon.

And the calm moonlight seems to say:
*Hast thou then still the old unquiet breast,*
*Which neither deadens into rest,*
*Nor ever feels the fiery glow*
*That whirls the spirit from itself away,*
*But fluctuates to and fro,*
*Never by passion quite possess'd*
*And never quite benumb'd by the world's sway?—*
And I, I know not if to pray
Still to be what I am, or yield and be
Like all the other men I see.

For most men in a brazen prison live,
Where, in the sun's hot eye,
With heads bent o'er their toil, they languidly
Their lives to some unmeaning taskwork give,
Dreaming of nought beyond their prison-wall.
And as, year after year,
Fresh products of their barren labour fall
From their tired hands, and rest
Never yet comes more near,
Gloom settles slowly down over their breast;

And while they try to stem
The waves of mournful thought by which they are prest,
Death in their prison reaches them,
Unfreed, having seen nothing, still unblest. 50

And the rest, a few,
Escape their prison and depart
On the wide ocean of life anew.
There the freed prisoner, where'er his heart
Listeth, will sail; 55
Nor doth he know how there prevail,
Despotic on that sea,
Trade-winds which cross it from eternity.
Awhile he holds some false way, undebarr'd
By thwarting signs, and braves 60
The freshening wind and blackening waves.
And then the tempest strikes him; and between
The lightning-bursts is seen
Only a driving wreck,
And the pale master on his spar-strewn deck 65
With anguish'd face and flying hair
Grasping the rudder hard,
Still bent to make some port he knows not where,
Still standing for some false, impossible shore.
And sterner comes the roar 70
Of sea and wind, and through the deepening gloom
Fainter and fainter wreck and helmsman loom,
And he too disappears, and comes no more.

Is there no life, but these alone?
Madman or slave, must man be one? 75

Plainness and clearness without shadow of stain!
Clearness divine!

Ye heavens, whose pure dark regions have no sign
Of languor, though so calm, and, though so great,
Are yet untroubled and unpassionate;  80
Who, though so noble, share in the world's toil,
And, though so task'd, keep free from dust and soil!
I will not say that your mild deeps retain
A tinge, it may be, of their silent pain
Who have long'd deeply once, and long'd in vain—  85
But I will rather say that you remain
A world above man's head, to let him see
How boundless might his soul's horizons be,
How vast, yet of what clear transparency!
How it were good to abide there, and breathe free;  90
How fair a lot to fill
Is left to each man still!


## LINES

#### WRITTEN IN KENSINGTON GARDENS

In this lone, open glade I lie,
Screen'd by deep boughs on either hand;
And at its end, to stay the eye,
Those black-crown'd, red-boled pine-trees stand!

Birds here make song, each bird has his,  5
Across the girdling city's hum.
How green under the boughs it is!
How thick the tremulous sheep-cries come!

Sometimes a child will cross the glade
To take his nurse his broken toy;  10
Sometimes a thrush flit overhead
Deep in her unknown day's employ.

Here at my feet what wonders pass,
What endless, active life is here!
What blowing daisies, fragrant grass!  15
An air-stirred forest, fresh and clear

Scarce fresher is the mountain-sod
Where the tired angler lies, stretch'd out,
And, eased of basket and of rod,
Counts his day's spoil, the spotted trout.  20

In the huge world, which roars hard by,
Be others happy if they can!
But in my helpless cradle I
Was breathed on by the rural Pan.

I, on men's impious uproar hurl'd,  25
Think often, as I hear them rave,
That peace has left the upper world
And now keeps only in the grave.

Yet here is peace for ever new!
When I who watch them am away,  30
Still all things in this glade go through
The changes of their quiet day.

Then to their happy rest they pass!
The flowers upclose, the birds are fed,
The night comes down upon the grass,  35
The child sleeps warmly in his bed.

Calm soul of all things! make it mine
To feel, amid the city's jar,
That there abides a peace of thine,
Man did not make, and cannot mar.  40

The will to neither strive nor cry,
The power to feel with others give!
Calm, calm me more! nor let me die
Before I have begun to live.


## THE FUTURE

A WANDERER is man from his birth.
He was born in a ship
On the breast of the river of Time;
Brimming with wonder and joy
He spreads out his arms to the light, 5
Rivets his gaze on the banks of the stream.

As what he sees is, so have his thoughts been.
Whether he wakes,
Where the snowy mountainous pass,
Echoing the screams of the eagles, 10
Hems in its gorges the bed
Of the new-born clear-flowing stream;
Whether he first sees light
Where the river in gleaming rings
Sluggishly winds through the plain; 15
Whether in sound of the swallowing sea—
As is the world on the banks,
So is the mind of the man.

  Vainly does each, as he glides,
Fable and dream 20
Of the lands which the river of Time
Had left ere he woke on its breast,
Or shall reach when his eyes have been closed.

Only the tract where he sails
He wots of; only the thoughts,            25
Raised by the objects he passes, are his.

Who can see the green earth any more
As she was by the sources of Time?
Who imagines her fields as they lay
In the sunshine, unworn by the plough?   30
Who thinks as they thought,
The tribes who then roam'd on her breast,
Her vigorous, primitive sons?

What girl
Now reads in her bosom as clear          35
As Rebekah read, when she sate
At eve by the palm-shaded well?
Who guards in her breast
As deep, as pellucid a spring
Of feeling, as tranquil, as sure?        40

  What bard,
At the height of his vision, can deem
Of God, of the world, of the soul,
With a plainness as near,
As flashing as Moses felt                45
When he lay in the night by his flock
On the starlit Arabian waste?
Can rise and obey
The beck of the Spirit like him?

This tract which the river of Time       50
Now flows through with us, is the plain.
Gone is the calm of its earlier shore.
Border'd by cities and hoarse

With a thousand cries is its stream
And we on its breast, our minds
Are confused as the cries which we hear,
Changing and shot as the sights which we see.

And we say that repose has fled
For ever the course of the river of Time.
That cities will crowd to its edge
In a blacker, incessanter line;
That the din will be more on its banks,
Denser the trade on its stream,
Flatter the plain where it flows,
Fiercer the sun overhead.
That never will those on its breast
See an ennobling sight,
Drink of the feeling of quiet again.

But what was before us we know not,
And we know not what shall succeed.

Haply, the river of Time—
As it grows, as the towns on its marge
Fling their wavering lights
On a wider, statelier stream—
May acquire, if not the calm
Of its early mountainous shore,
Yet a solemn peace of its own.

And the width of the waters, the hush
Of the grey expanse where he floats,
Freshening its current and spotted with foam
As it draws to the Ocean, may strike
Peace to the soul of the man on its breast—
As the pale waste widens around him,

As the banks fade dimmer away,
As the stars come out, and the night-wind
Brings up the stream
Murmurs and scents of the infinite sea.


## THE SCHOLAR-GIPSY

Go, for they call you, shepherd, from the hill;
  Go, shepherd, and untie the wattled cotes!
    No longer leave thy wistful flock unfed,
  Nor let thy bawling fellows rack their throats,
    Nor the cropp'd herbage shoot another head.     5
      But when the fields are still,
  And the tired men and dogs all gone to rest,
    And only the white sheep are sometimes seen
    Cross and recross the strips of moon-blanch'd green,
  Come, shepherd, and again begin the quest!     10

Here, where the reaper was at work of late—
  In this high field's dark corner, where he leaves
    His coat, his basket, and his earthen cruse,
  And in the sun all morning binds the sheaves,
    Then here, at noon, comes back his stores to use—
      Here will I sit and wait,     16
  While to my ear from uplands far away
    The bleating of the folded flocks is borne,
    With distant cries of reapers in the corn—
  All the live murmur of a summer's day.     20

Screen'd is this nook o'er the high, half-reap'd field,
  And here till sun-down, shepherd! will I be.
    Through the thick corn the scarlet poppies peep,
  And round green roots and yellowing stalks I see

Pale pink convolvulus in tendrils creep;  25
  And air-swept lindens yield
Their scent, and rustle down their perfumed showers
  Of bloom on the bent grass where I am laid,
  And bower me from the August sun with shade;
And the eye travels down to Oxford's towers.  30

And near me on the grass lies Glanvil's book—
  Come, let me read the oft-read tale again!
    The story of the Oxford scholar poor,
  Of pregnant parts and quick inventive brain,
    Who, tired of knocking at preferment's door,  35
      One summer-morn forsook
His friends, and went to learn the gipsy-lore,
  And roam'd the world with that wild brotherhood,
  And came, as most men deem'd, to little good,
But came to Oxford and his friends no more.  40

But once, years after, in the country-lanes,
  Two scholars, whom at college erst he knew,
    Met him, and of his way of life enquired;
  Whereat he answer'd, that the gipsy-crew,
    His mates, had arts to rule as they desired  45
      The workings of men's brains,
And they can bind them to what thoughts they will.
  "And I," he said, "the secret of their art,
  When fully learn'd, will to the world impart;
But it needs heaven-sent moments for this skill."  50

This said, he left them, and return'd no more—
  But rumours hung about the country-side,
    That the lost Scholar long was seen to stray,
  Seen by rare glimpses, pensive and tongue-tied,
    In hat of antique shape, and cloak of grey,  55

The same the gipsies wore.
Shepherds had met him on the Hurst in spring;
    At some lone alehouse in the Berkshire moors,
    On the warm ingle-bench, the smock-frock'd boors
Had found him seated at their entering,                60

But, 'mid their drink and clatter, he would fly.
    And I myself seem half to know thy looks,
        And put the shepherds, wanderer! on thy trace;
    And boys who in lone wheatfields scare the rooks
        I ask if thou hast pass'd their quiet place;    65
            Or in my boat I lie
    Moor'd to the cool bank in the summer-heats,
        'Mid wide grass meadows which the sunshine fills,
        And watch the warm, green-muffled Cumner hills,
    And wonder if thou haunt'st their shy retreats.    70

For most, I know, thou lov'st retired ground!
    Thee at the ferry Oxford riders blithe,
        Returning home on summer-nights, have met
    Crossing the stripling Thames at Bab-lock-hithe,
        Trailing in the cool stream thy fingers wet,    75
            As the punt's rope chops round;
    And leaning backward in a pensive dream,
        And fostering in thy lap a heap of flowers
        Pluck'd in shy fields and distant Wychwood bowers,
    And thine eyes resting on the moonlit stream.    80

And then they land, and thou art seen no more!—
    Maidens, who from the distant hamlets come
        To dance around the Fyfield elm in May,
    Oft through the darkening fields have seen thee roam,
        Or cross a stile into the public way.          85

Oft thou hast given them store
Of flowers—the frail-leaf'd, white anemony,
Dark bluebells drench'd with dews of summer eves,
And purple orchises with spotted leaves—
But none hath words she can report of thee. 90

And, above Godstow Bridge, when hay-time's here
In June, and many a scythe in sunshine flames,
Men who through those wide fields of breezy grass
Where black-wing'd swallows haunt the glittering Thames,
To bathe in the abandon'd lasher pass, 95
Have often pass'd thee near
Sitting upon the river bank o'ergrown;
Mark'd thine outlandish garb, thy figure spare,
Thy dark vague eyes, and soft abstracted air—
But, when they came from bathing, thou wast gone!

At some lone homestead in the Cumner hills, 101
Where at her open door the housewife darns,
Thou hast been seen, or hanging on a gate
To watch the threshers in the mossy barns.
Children, who early range these slopes and late 105
For cresses from the rills,
Have known thee eying, all an April-day,
The springing pastures and the feeding kine;
And mark'd thee, when the stars come out and shine,
Through the long dewy grass move slow away. 110

In autumn, on the skirts of Bagley Wood—
Where most the gipsies by the turf-edged way
Pitch their smoked tents, and every bush you see
With scarlet patches tagg'd and shreds of grey,
Above the forest-ground called Thessaly— 115

>     The blackbird, picking food,
>   Sees thee, nor stops his meal, nor fears at all;
>     So often has he known thee past him stray,
>     Rapt, twirling in thy hand a wither'd spray,
>   And waiting for the spark from heaven to fall. 120
>
> And once, in winter, on the causeway chill
>   Where home through flooded fields foot-travellers go,
>     Have I not pass'd thee on the wooden bridge,
>   Wrapt in thy cloak and battling with the snow,
>     Thy face tow'rd Hinksey and its wintry ridge? 125
>       And thou hast climb'd the hill,
>   And gain'd the white brow of the Cumner range;
>     Turn'd once to watch, while thick the snowflakes fall,
>     The line of festal light in Christ-Church hall—
>   Then sought thy straw in some sequester'd grange. 130
>
> But what—I dream! Two hundred years are flown
>   Since first thy story ran through Oxford halls,
>     And the grave Glanvil did the tale inscribe
>   That thou wert wander'd from the studious walls
>     To learn strange arts, and join a gipsy-tribe; 135
>       And thou from earth art gone
>   Long since, and in some quiet churchyard laid—
>     Some country-nook, where o'er thy unknown grave
>     Tall grasses and white flowering nettles wave,
>   Under a dark, red-fruited yew-tree's shade. 140
>
> —No, no, thou hast not felt the lapse of hours!
>   For what wears out the life of mortal men?
>     'Tis that from change to change their being rolls;
>   'Tis that repeated shocks, again, again,
>     Exhaust the energy of strongest souls 145
>       And numb the elastic powers.

Till having used our nerves with bliss and teen,
  And tired upon a thousand schemes our wit,
  To the just-pausing Genius we remit
Our worn-out life, and are—what we have been.   150

Thou hast not lived, why should'st thou perish, so?
  Thou hadst *one* aim, *one* business, *one* desire;
    Else wert thou long since number'd with the dead!
  Else hadst thou spent, like other men, thy fire!
    The generations of thy peers are fled,   155
      And we ourselves shall go;
  But thou possessest an immortal lot,
    And we imagine thee exempt from age
    And living as thou liv'st on Glanvil's page,
  Because thou hadst—what we, alas! have not.   160

For early didst thou leave the world, with powers
  Fresh, undiverted to the world without,
    Firm to their mark, not spent on other things;
  Free from the sick fatigue, the languid doubt,
    Which much to have tried, in much been baffled, brings.
      O life unlike to ours!   166
  Who fluctuate idly without term or scope,
    Of whom each strives, nor knows for what he strives,
    And each half lives a hundred different lives;
  Who wait like thee, but not, like thee, in hope.   170

Thou waitest for the spark from heaven! and we,
  Light half-believers of our casual creeds,
    Who never deeply felt, nor clearly will'd,
  Whose insight never has borne fruit in deeds,
    Whose vague resolves never have been fulfill'd;   175
      For whom each year we see
  Breeds new beginnings, disappointments new;

Who hesitate and falter life away,
And lose to-morrow the ground won to-day—
Ah! do not we, wanderer! await it too?  180

Yes, we await it!—but it still delays,
And then we suffer! and amongst us one,
Who most has suffer'd, takes dejectedly
His seat upon the intellectual throne;
And all his store of sad experience he  185
Lays bare of wretched days;
Tells us his misery's birth and growth and signs,
And how the dying spark of hope was fed,
And how the breast was soothed, and how the head,
And all his hourly varied anodynes.  190

This for our wisest! and we others pine,
And wish the long unhappy dream would end,
And waive all claim to bliss, and try to bear;
With close-lipp'd patience for our only friend,
Sad patience, too near neighbour to despair—  195
But none has hope like thine!
Thou through the fields and through the woods dost stray,
Roaming the country-side, a truant boy,
Nursing thy project in unclouded joy,
And every doubt long blown by time away.  200

O born in days when wits were fresh and clear,
And life ran gaily as the sparkling Thames;
Before this strange disease of modern life,
With its sick hurry, its divided aims,
Its heads o'ertax'd, its palsied hearts, was rife—  205
Fly hence, our contact fear!
Still fly, plunge deeper in the bowering wood!
Averse, as Dido did with gesture stern

From her false friend's approach in Hades turn,
Wave us away, and keep thy solitude!

Still nursing the unconquerable hope,
  Still clutching the inviolable shade,
    With a free, onward impulse brushing through,
  By night, the silver'd branches of the glade—
    Far on the forest-skirts, where none pursue,
      On some mild pastoral slope
    Emerge, and resting on the moonlit pales
    Freshen thy flowers as in former years
    With dew, or listen with enchanted ears,
  From the dark dingles, to the nightingales!

But fly our paths, our feverish contact fly!
  For strong the infection of our mental strife,
    Which, though it gives no bliss, yet spoils for rest;
  And we should win thee from thy own fair life,
    Like us distracted, and like us unblest.
      Soon, soon thy cheer would die,
    Thy hopes grow timorous, and unfix'd thy powers,
    And thy clear aims be cross and shifting made;
    And then thy glad perennial youth would fade,
  Fade, and grow old at last, and die like ours.

Then fly our greetings, fly our speech and smiles!
  —As some grave Tyrian trader, from the sea,
    Descried at sunrise an emerging prow
  Lifting the cool-hair'd creepers stealthily,
    The fringes of a southward-facing brow
      Among the Ægæan isles;
    And saw the merry Grecian coaster come,
    Freighted with amber grapes, and Chian wine,

    Green, bursting figs, and tunnies steep'd in brine—
    And knew the intruders on his ancient home,           240

The young light-hearted masters of the waves—
  And snatch'd his rudder, and shook out more sail;
    And day and night held on indignantly
  O'er the blue Midland waters with the gale,
    Betwixt the Syrtes and soft Sicily,                  245
      To where the Atlantic raves
  Outside the western straits;   and unbent sails
    There, where down cloudy cliffs, through sheets of foam,
    Shy traffickers, the dark Iberians come;
  And on the beach undid his corded bales.               250


## THYRSIS

*A* MONODY, *to commemorate the author's friend,*

ARTHUR HUGH CLOUGH, *who died at Florence,* 1861.

How changed is here each spot man makes or fills!
  In the two Hinkseys nothing keeps the same;
    The village street its haunted mansion lacks,
  And from the sign is gone Sibylla's name,
    And from the roofs the twisted chimney-stacks—       5
      Are ye too changed, ye hills?
  See, 'tis no foot of unfamiliar men
    To-night from Oxford up your pathway strays!
    Here came I often, often, in old days—
  Thyrsis and I; we still had Thyrsis then.              10

Runs it not here, the track by Childsworth Farm,
  Past the high wood, to where the elm-tree crowns
    The hill behind whose ridge the sunset flames?

The signal-elm that looks on Ilsley Downs,
　　The Vale, the three lone weirs, the youthful Thames?—
　　　This winter-eve is warm,
Humid the air! leafless, yet soft as spring,
　　The tender purple spray on copse and briers!
　　And that sweet city with her dreaming spires,
She needs not June for beauty's heightening,

Lovely all times she lies, lovely to-night!—
　　Only, methinks, some loss of habit's power
　　Befalls me wandering through this upland dim.
　　Once pass'd I blindfold here, at any hour;
　　Now seldom come I, since I came with him.
　　　That single elm-tree bright
　　Against the west—I miss it! is it gone?
　　We prized it dearly; while it stood, we said,
　　Our friend, the Gipsy-Scholar, was not dead;
While the tree lived, he in these fields lived on.

Too rare, too rare, grow now my visits here,
　　But once I knew each field, each flower, each stick;
　　And with the country-folk acquaintance made
　　By barn in threshing-time, by new-built rick.
　　Here, too, our shepherd-pipes we first assay'd.
　　　Ah me! this many a year
　　My pipe is lost, my shepherd's holiday!
　　Needs must I lose them, needs with heavy heart
　　Into the world and wave of men depart;
But Thyrsis of his own will went away.

It irk'd him to be here, he could not rest.
　　He loved each simple joy the country yields,
　　　He loved his mates; but yet he could not keep,
　　For that a shadow lour'd on the fields,

Here with the shepherds and the silly sheep. 45
    Some life of men unblest
He knew, which made him droop, and fill'd his head.
    He went; his piping took a troubled sound
    Of storms that rage outside our happy ground;
He could not wait their passing, he is dead. 50

So, some tempestuous morn in early June,
    When the year's primal burst of bloom is o'er,
    Before the roses and the longest day—
    When garden-walks and all the grassy floor
    With blossoms red and white of fallen May 55
    And chestnut-flowers are strewn—
So have I heard the cuckoo's parting cry,
    From the wet field, through the vext garden-trees,
    Come with the volleying rain and tossing breeze:
*The bloom is gone, and with the bloom go I!* 60

Too quick despairer, wherefore wilt thou go?
    Soon will the high Midsummer pomps come on,
    Soon will the musk carnations break and swell,
    Soon shall we have gold-dusted snapdragon,
    Sweet-William with his homely cottage-smell, 65
    And stocks in fragrant blow;
Roses that down the alleys shine afar.
    And open, jasmine-muffled lattices,
    And groups under the dreaming garden-trees,
And the full moon, and the white evening-star. 70

He hearkens not! light comer, he is flown!
    What matters it? next year he will return,
    And we shall have him in the sweet spring-days,
    With whitening hedges, and uncrumpling fern,
    And blue-bells trembling by the forest-ways, 75

    And scent of hay new-mown.
  But Thyrsis never more we swains shall see;
    See him come back, and cut a smoother reed,
    And blow a strain the world at last shall heed—
  For Time, not Corydon, hath conquer'd thee!    80

Alack, for Corydon no rival now!—
  But when Sicilian shepherds lost a mate,
    Some good survivor with his flute would go,
  Piping a ditty sad for Bion's fate;
    And cross the unpermitted ferry's flow,    85
      And relax Pluto's brow,
  And make leap up with joy the beauteous head
    Of Proserpine, among whose crowned hair
    Are flowers first open'd on Sicilian air,
  And flute his friend, like Orpheus, from the dead.    90

O easy access to the hearer's grace
  When Dorian shepherds sang to Proserpine.
    For she herself had trod Sicilian fields,
  She knew the Dorian water's gush divine,
    She knew each lily white which Enna yields,    95
      Each rose with blushing face;
  She loved the Dorian pipe, the Dorian strain.
    But ah, of our poor Thames she never heard!
    Her foot the Cumner cowslips never stirr'd;
  And we should tease her with our plaint in vain!    100

Well! wind-dispersed and vain the words will be,
  Yet, Thyrsis, let me give my grief its hour
    In the old haunt, and find our tree-topp'd hill!
  Who, if not I, for questing here hath power?
    I know the wood which hides the daffodil,    105
      I know the Fyfield tree,

I know what white, what purple fritillaries
   The grassy harvest of the river-fields,
   Above by Ensham, down by Sandford, yields,
And what sedged brooks are Thames's tributaries;   110

I know these slopes; who knows them if not I?—
   But many a dingle on the loved hill-side,
     With thorns once studded, old, white-blossom'd trees,
   Where thick the cowslips grew, and far descried
     High tower'd the spikes of purple orchises,   115
       Hath since our day put by
   The coronals of that forgotten time;
     Down each green bank hath gone the ploughboy's team,
     And only in the hidden brookside gleam
Primroses, orphans of the flowery prime.   120

Where is the girl, who by the boatman's door,
   Above the locks, above the boating throng,
     Unmoor'd our skiff when through the Wytham flats,
   Red loosestrife and blond meadow-sweet among
     And darting swallows and light water-gnats,   125
       We track'd the shy Thames shore?
   Where are the mowers, who, as the tiny swell
     Of our boat passing heaved the river-grass,
     Stood with suspended scythe to see us pass?—
They all are gone, and thou art gone as well!   130

Yes, thou art gone! and round me too the night
   In ever-nearing circle weaves her shade.
     I see her veil draw soft across the day,
   I feel her slowly chilling breath invade
     The cheek grown thin, the brown hair sprent with grey;
       I feel her finger light   136
   Laid pausefully upon life's headlong train;—

The foot less prompt to meet the morning dew,
The heart less bounding at emotion new,
And hope, once crush'd, less quick to spring again.  140

And long the way appears, which seem'd so short
To the less practised eye of sanguine youth;
And high the mountain-tops, in cloudy air,
The mountain-tops where is the throne of Truth,
Tops in life's morning-sun so bright and bare!  145
Unbreachable the fort
Of the long-batter'd world uplifts its wall;
And strange and vain the earthly turmoil grows,
And near and real the charm of thy repose,
And night as welcome as a friend would fall.  150

But hush! the upland hath a sudden loss
Of quiet!—Look, adown the dusk hill-side,
A troop of Oxford hunters going home,
As in old days, jovial and talking, ride!
From hunting with the Berkshire hounds they come.
Quick! let me fly, and cross  156
Into yon farther field!—'Tis done; and see,
Back'd by the sunset, which doth glorify
The orange and pale violet evening sky,
Bare on its lonely ridge, the Tree! the Tree!  160

I take the omen! Eve lets down her veil,
The white fog creeps from bush to bush about,
The west unflushes, the high stars grow bright,
And in the scatter'd farms the lights come out.
I cannot reach the signal-tree to-night,  165
Yet, happy omen, hail!
Hear it from thy broad lucent Arno-vale
(For there thine earth-forgetting eyelids keep

The morningless and unawakening sleep
   Under the flowery oleanders pale),                170

Hear it, O Thyrsis, still our tree is there!—
   Ah, vain! These English fields, this upland dim,
   These brambles pale with mist engarlanded,
   That lone, sky-pointing tree, are not for him;
      To a boon southern country he is fled,        175
         And now in happier air,
   Wandering with the great Mother's train divine
      (And purer or more subtle soul than thee,
      I trow, the mighty Mother doth not see)
   Within a folding of the Apennine,                180

Thou hearest the immortal chants of old!—
   Putting his sickle to the perilous grain
      In the hot cornfield of the Phrygian king,
   For thee the Lityerses-song again
      Young Daphnis with his silver voice doth sing;  185
         Sings his Sicilian fold,
   His sheep, his hapless love, his blinded eyes—
      And how a call celestial round him rang,
      And heavenward from the fountain-brink he sprang,
   And all the marvel of the golden skies.          190

There thou are gone, and me thou leavest here
   Sole in these fields! yet will I not despair.
      Despair I will not, while I yet descry
   Neath the mild canopy of English air
      That lonely tree against the western sky.     195
         Still, still these slopes, 'tis clear,
   Our Gipsy-Scholar haunts, outliving thee!
      Fields where soft sheep from cages pull the hay,

Woods with anemonies in flower till May,
Know him a wanderer still; then why not me? 200

A fugitive and gracious light he seeks,
Shy to illumine; and I seek it too.
This does not come with houses or with gold,
With place, with honour, and a flattering crew;
'Tis not in the world's market bought and sold—
But the smooth-slipping weeks 236
Drop by, and leave its seeker still untired;
Out of the heed of mortals he is gone,
He wends unfollow'd, he must house alone;
Yet on he fares, by his own heart inspired. 210

Thou too, O Thyrsis, on like quest wast bound;
Thou wanderedst with me for a little hour!
Men gave thee nothing; but this happy quest,
If men esteem'd thee feeble, gave thee power,
If men procured thee trouble, gave thee rest. 215
And this rude Cumner ground,
Its fir-topped Hurst, its farms, its quiet fields,
Here cam'st thou in thy jocund youthful time,
Here was thine height of strength, thy golden prime!
And still the haunt beloved a virtue yields. 220

What though tne music of thy rustic flute
Kept not for long its happy, country tone;
Lost it too soon, and learnt a stormy note
Of men contention-tost, of men who groan,
Which task'd thy pipe too sore, and tired thy throat—
It fail'd, and thou wast mute! 226
Yet hadst thou alway visions of our light,
And long with men of care thou couldst not stay,

And soon thy foot resumed its wandering way,
Left human haunt, and on alone till night.     230

Too rare, too rare, grow now my visits here!
  'Mid city-noise, not, as with thee of yore,
    Thyrsis! in reach of sheep-bells is my home.
  —Then through the great town's harsh, heart-wearying
      roar,
    Let in thy voice a whisper often come,     235
      To chase fatigue and fear:
*Why faintest thou? I wander'd till I died.*
  *Roam on! The light we sought is shining still.*
  *Dost thou ask proof? Our tree yet crowns the hill,*
*Our Scholar travels yet the loved hill-side.*     240


## MEMORIAL VERSES

### April, 1850

GOETHE in Weimar sleeps, and Greece,
Long since, saw Byron's struggle cease.
But one such death remain'd to come;
The last poetic voice is dumb—
We stand to-day by Wordsworth's tomb.     5

When Byron's eyes were shut in death,
We bow'd our head and held our breath.
He taught us little; but our soul
Had *felt* him like the thunder's roll.
With shivering heart the strife we saw     10
Of passion with eternal law;
And yet with reverential awe
We watch'd the fount of fiery life
Which served for that Titanic strife.

When Goethe's death was told, we said:
Sunk, then, is Europe's sagest head.
Physician of the iron age,
Goethe has done his pilgrimage.
He took the suffering human race,
He read each wound, each weakness clear;
And struck his finger on the place,
And said: *Thou ailest here, and here!*
He look'd on Europe's dying hour
Of fitful dream and feverish power;
His eye plunged down the weltering strife,
The turmoil of expiring life—
He said: *The end is everywhere,*
*Art still has truth, take refuge there!*
And he was happy, if to know
Causes of things, and far below
His feet to see the lurid flow
Of terror, and insane distress,
And headlong fate, be happiness.

And Wordsworth!—Ah, pale ghosts, rejoice!
For never has such soothing voice
Been to your shadowy world convey'd,
Since erst, at morn, some wandering shade
Heard the clear song of Orpheus come
Through Hades, and the mournful gloom.
Wordsworth has gone from us—and ye,
Ah, may ye feel his voice as we!
He too upon a wintry clime
Had fallen—on this iron time
Of doubts, disputes, distractions, fears.
He found us when the age had bound
Our souls in its benumbing round;

He spoke, and loosed our heart in tears.
He laid us as we lay at birth
On the cool flowery lap of earth,
Smiles broke from us and we had ease;  50
The hills were round us, and the breeze
Went o'er the sun-lit fields again;
Our foreheads felt the wind, and rain.
Our youth return'd; for there was shed
On spirits that had long been dead,  55
Spirits dried up and closely furl'd,
The freshness of the early world.

Ah! since dark days still bring to light
Man's prudence and man's fiery might,
Time may restore us in his course  60
Goethe's sage mind and Byron's force;
But where will Europe's latter hour
Again find Wordsworth's healing power?
Others will teach us how to dare,
And against fear our breast to steel;  65
Others will strengthen us to bear—
But who, ah! who, will make us feel?
The cloud of mortal destiny,
Others will front it fearlessly—
But who, like him, will put it by?  70

Keep fresh the grass upon his grave
O Rotha, with thy living wave!
Sing him thy best! for few or none
Hears thy voice right, now he is gone.

## A SOUTHERN NIGHT

THE sandy spits, the shore-lock'd lakes,
  Melt into open, moonlit sea;
The soft Mediterranean breaks
    At my feet, free.

Dotting the fields of corn and vine,
  Like ghosts the huge, gnarl'd olives stand
Behind, that lovely mountain-line!
    While, by the strand,

Cette, with its glistening houses white,
  Curves with the curving beach away
To where the lighthouse beacons bright
    Far in the bay.

Ah! such a night, so soft, so lone,
  So moonlit, saw me once of yore
Wander unquiet, and my own
    Vext heart deplore.

But now that trouble is forgot;
  Thy memory, thy pain, to-night,
My brother! and thine early lot,
    Possess me quite.

The murmur of this Midland deep
  Is heard to-night around thy grave,
There, where Gibraltar's cannon'd steep
    O'erfrowns the wave.

For there, with bodily anguish keen, 25
  With Indian heats at last fordone,
With public toil and private teen—
    Thou sank'st, alone.

Slow to a stop, at morning grey,
  I see the smoke-crown'd vessel come; 30
Slow round her paddles dies away
    The seething foam.

A boat is lower'd from her side;
  Ah, gently place him on the bench!
That spirit—if all have not yet died— 35
    A breath might quench.

Is this the eye, the footstep fast,
  The mien of youth we used to see,
Poor, gallant boy!—for such thou wast,
    Still art, to me. 40

The limbs their wonted tasks refuse;
  The eyes are glazed, thou canst not speak;
And whiter than thy white burnous
    That wasted cheek!

Enough! The boat, with quiet shock, 45
  Unto its haven coming nigh,
Touches, and on Gibraltar's rock
    Lands thee to die.

Ah me! Gibraltar's strand is far,
  But farther yet across the brine 50
Thy dear wife's ashes buried are,
    Remote from thine.

For there, where morning's sacred fount
   Its golden rain on earth confers,
The snowy Himalayan Mount
      O'ershadows hers.

Strange irony of fate, alas,
   Which, for two jaded English, saves,
When from their dusty life they pass,
      Such peaceful graves!

In cities should we English lie,
   Where cries are rising ever new,
And men's incessant stream goes by—
      We who pursue

Our business with unslackening stride,
   Traverse in troops, with care-fill'd breast,
The soft Mediterranean side,
      The Nile, the East,

And see all sights from pole to pole,
   And glance, and nod, and bustle by,
And never once possess our soul
      Before we die.

Not by those hoary Indian hills,
   Not by this gracious Midland sea
Whose floor to-night sweet moonshine fills,
      Should our graves be.

Some sage, to whom the world was dead,
   And men were specks, and life a play;
Who made the roots of trees his bed,
      And once a day

With staff and gourd his way did bend
  To villages and homes of man,
For food to keep him till he end
    His mortal span

And the pure goal of being reach;           85
  Hoar-headed, wrinkled, clad in white,
Without companion, without speech,
    By day and night

Pondering God's mysteries untold,
  And tranquil as the glacier-snows,        90
He by those Indian mountains old
    Might well repose.

Some grey crusading knight austere,
  Who bore Saint Louis company,
And came home hurt to death, and here       95
    Landed to die;

Some youthful troubadour, whose tongue
  Fill'd Europe once with his love-pain,
Who here outworn had sunk, and sung
    His dying strain;                       100

Some girl, who here from castle-bower,
  With furtive step and cheek of flame,
'Twixt myrtle-hedges all in flower
    By moonlight came

To meet her pirate-lover's ship;            105
  And from the wave-kiss'd marble stair
Beckon'd him on, with quivering lip
    And floating hair:

## A SOUTHERN NIGHT

And lived some moons in happy trance,
    Then learnt his death and pined away—    110
Such by these waters of romance
    'Twas meet to lay.

But you—a grave for knight or sage,
    Romantic, solitary, still,
O spent ones of a work-day age!    115
    Befits you ill.

So sang I; but the midnight breeze,
    Down to the brimm'd, moon-charmed main
Comes softly through the olive-trees,    120
    And checks my strain.

I think of her, whose gentle tongue
    All plaint in her own cause controll'd;
Of thee I think, my brother! young
    In heart, high-soul'd—

That comely face, that cluster'd brow,    125
    That cordial hand, that bearing free,
I see them still, I see them now,
    Shall always see!

And what but gentleness untired,
    And what but noble feeling warm,    130
Whenever shown, howe'er inspired,
    Is grace, is charm?

What else is all these waters are,
    What else is steep'd in lucid sheen,
What else is bright, what else is fair,    135
    What else serene?

Mild o'er her grave, ye mountains, shine!
  Gently by his, ye waters, glide!
To that in you which is divine
    They were allied.          140


## RUGBY CHAPEL

### NOVEMBER, 1857

COLDLY, sadly descends
The autumn-evening. The field
Strewn with its dank yellow drifts
Of wither'd leaves, and the elms,
Fade into dimness apace,         5
Silent;—hardly a shout
From a few boys late at their play!
The lights come out in the street,
In the school-room windows;—but cold,
Solemn, unlighted, austere,        10
Through the gathering darkness, arise
The chapel-walls, in whose bound
Thou, my father! art laid.

There thou dost lie, in the gloom
Of the autumn evening. But ah!        15
That word, *gloom*, to my mind
Brings thee back, in the light
Of thy radiant vigour, again;
In the gloom of November we pass'd
Days not dark at thy side;        20
Seasons impair'd not the ray
Of thy bouyant cheerfulness clear.
Such thou wast! and I stand

In the autumn evening, and think
Of bygone autumns with thee.

Fifteen years have gone round
Since thou arosest to tread,
In the summer-morning, the road
Of death, at a call unforseen,
Sudden.  For fifteen years,
We who till then in thy shade
Rested as under the boughs
Of a mighty oak, have endured
Sunshine and rain as we might,
Bare, unshaded, alone,
Lacking the shelter of thee.

O strong soul, by what shore
Tarriest thou now?  For that force,
Surely, has not been left vain!
Somewhere, surely, afar,
In the sounding labour-house vast
Of being, is practised that strength,
Zealous, beneficent, firm!

Yes, in some far-shining sphere,
Conscious or not of the past,
Still thou performest the word
Of the Spirit in whom thou dost live—
Prompt, unwearied, as here!
Still thou upraisest with zeal
The humble good from the ground,
Sternly repressest the bad!
Still, like a trumpet, dost rouse
Those who with half-open eyes
Tread the border-land dim

'Twixt vice and virtue; reviv'st, 55
Succourest!—this was thy work,
This was thy life upon earth.

What is the course of the life
Of mortal men on the earth?—
Most men eddy about 60
Here and there—eat and drink,
Chatter and love and hate,
Gather and squander, are raised
Aloft, are hurl'd in the dust,
Striving blindly, achieving 65
Nothing; and then they die—
Perish;—and no one asks
Who or what they have been,
More than he asks what waves,
In the moonlit solitudes mild 70
Of the midmost Ocean, have swell'd,
Foam'd for a moment, and gone.

And there are some, whom a thirst
Ardent, unquenchable, fires,
Not with the crowd to be spent, 75
Not without aim to go round
In an eddy of purposeless dust,
Effort unmeaning and vain.
Ah yes! some of us strive
Not without action to die 80
Fruitless, but something to snatch
From dull oblivion, nor all
Glut the devouring grave!
We, we have chosen our path—
Path to a clear-purposed goal, 85
Path of advance!—but it leads

A long, steep journey, through sunk
Gorges, o'er mountains in snow.
Cheerful, with friends, we set forth—
Then, on the height, comes the storm.  90
Thunder crashes from rock
To rock, the cataracts reply,
Lightnings dazzle our eyes.
Roaring torrents have breach'd
The track, the stream-bed descends  95
In the place where the wayfarer once
Planted his footstep—the spray
Boils o'er its borders! aloft
The unseen snow-beds dislodge
Their hanging ruin; alas,  100
Havoc is made in our train!
Friends who set forth at our side,
Falter, are lost in the storm.
We, we only are left!
With frowning foreheads, with lips  105
Sternly compress'd, we strain on,
On—and at nightfall at last
Come to the end of our way,
To the lonely inn 'mid the rocks;
Where the gaunt and taciturn host  110
Stands on the threshold, the wind
Shaking his thin white hairs—
Holds his lantern to scan
Our storm-beat figures, and asks:
Whom in our party we bring?  115
Whom we have left in the snow?

Sadly we answer: We bring
Only ourselves! we lost

Sight of the rest in the storm.
Hardly ourselves we fought through, 120
Stripp'd, without friends, as we are.
Friends, companions, and train,
The avalanche swept from our side.

But thou would'st not *alone*
Be saved, my father! *alone* 125
Conquer and come to thy goal,
Leaving the rest in the wild.
We were weary, and we
Fearful, and we in our march
Fain to drop down and to die. 130
Still thou turnedst, and still
Beckonedst the trembler, and still
Gavest the weary thy hand.

If, in the paths of the world,
Stones might have wounded thy feet, 135
Toil or dejection have tried
Thy spirit, of that we saw
Nothing—to us thou wast still
Cheerful, and helpful, and firm!
Therefore to thee it was given 140
Many to save with thyself;
And, at the end of thy day,
O faithful shepherd! to come,
Bringing thy sheep in thy hand.
And through thee I believe 145
In the noble and great who are gone;
Pure souls honour'd and blest
By former ages, who else—
Such, so soulless, so poor,

Is the race of men whom I see— 150
Seem'd but a dream of the heart,
Seem'd but a cry of desire.
Yes! I believe that there lived
Others like thee in the past,
Not like the men of the crowd 155
Who all round me to-day
Bluster or cringe, and make life
Hideous, and arid, and vile;
But souls temper'd with fire,
Fervent, heroic, and good, 160
Helpers and friends of mankind.

Servants of God!—or sons
Shall I not call you? because
Not as servants ye knew
Your Father's innermost mind, 165
His, who unwillingly sees
One of his little ones lost—
Yours is the praise, if mankind
Hath not as yet in its march
Fainted, and fallen, and died! 170

See! In the rocks of the world
Marches the host of mankind,
A feeble, wavering line.
Where are they tending?—A God
Marshall'd them, gave them their goal. 175
Ah, but the way is so long!
Years they have been in the wild!
Sore thirst plagues them, the rocks,
Rising all round, overawe;
Factions divide them, their host 180

Threatens to break, to dissolve.
—Ah, keep, keep them combined!
Else, of the myriads who fill
That army, not one shall arrive;
Sole they shall stray; in the rocks         185
Stagger for ever in vain,
Die one by one in the waste.

Then, in such hour of need
Of your fainting, dispirited race,
Ye, like angels, appear,                    190
Radiant with ardour divine!
Beacons of hope, ye appear!
Languor is not in your heart,
Weakness is not in your word,
Weariness not on your brow.                 195
Ye alight in our van! at your voice,
Panic, despair, flee away.
Ye move through the ranks, recall
The stragglers, refresh the outworn,
Praise, re-inspire the brave!               200
Order, courage, return.
Eyes rekindling, and prayers,
Follow your steps as ye go,
Ye fill up the gaps in our files,
Strengthen the wavering line,               205
Stablish, continue our march,
On, to the bound of the waste,
On, to the City of God.

## CALLICLES'S SONG

THROUGH the black, rushing smoke-bursts,
Thick breaks the red flame;
All Etna heaves fiercely
Her forest-clothed frame.

Not here, O Apollo!
Are haunts meet for thee.
But, where Helicon breaks down
In cliff to the sea,

Where the moon-silver'd inlets
Send far their light voice
Up the still vale of Thisbe,
O speed, and rejoice!

On the sward at the cliff-top
Lie strewn the white flocks,
On the cliff-side the pigeons
Roost deep in the rocks.

In the moonlight the shepherds,
Soft lull'd by the rills,
Lie wrapt in their blankets
Asleep on the hills.

—What forms are these coming
So white through the gloom?
What garments out-glistening
The gold-flower'd broom?

What sweet-breathing presence
Out-perfumes the thyme?
What voices enrapture
The night's balmy prime?—

'Tis Apollo comes leading
His choir, the Nine. 30
—The leader is fairest,
But all are divine.

They are lost in the hollows!
They stream up again!
What seeks on this mountain 35
The glorified train?—

They bathe on this mountain,
In the spring by their road;
Then on to Olympus,
Their endless abode. 40

—Whose praise do they mention?
Of what is it told?—
What will be for ever:
What was from of old.

First hymn they the Father 45
Of all things; and then,
The rest of immortals,
The action of men.

The day in his hotness,
The strife with the palm;
The night in her silence, 50
The stars in their calm.

# NOTES

## SOHRAB AND RUSTUM—(Page 3)

1. **And.** *And* is thus frequently used in the Bible to introduce an episode.

2. **Oxus.** Now called Amu Daria. It was the northeastern boundary of the Persian Empire. It rises in the Pamere tableland and flows northwest for 1300 miles, emptying into the Aral sea.

5. **he.** The pronoun would not be permitted in prose.

11. **Peran-Wisa** was a Turanian chief commanding the army of the Tartar King, Afrasiab.

15. **Pamere,** an extensive tableland in Central Asia, known as the "roof of the world."

38. **Afrasiab,** king of the Tartars, was one of the leading heroes of the Persian *Shah-Namah*.

40. **Samarcand,** a famous city of Turkestan, north of the Oxus.

42. **Ader-baijan,** or Azer-beijan, a province to the northwest of Persia, south of the European Caucasus, and east of the Caspian sea.

60. **common,** general.

82. **Seistan,** a province of Afghanistan bordering on Persia, and long held by Rustum's family as a fief to the Persian kings.

101. **Kara Kul,** a district near Bokhara.

113. **Casbin,** a city of Persia, just south of the *Elburz* mountains.

115. **frore,** frozen; from the Old English *froren*. Cf. *Paradise Regained*, III, 269-346.

119. **Bokhara,** a state of Central Asia, of which the capital, also named Bokhara, is the most important city.

120. **Khiva,** a Khanate, on the lower Oxus, bordering Bokhara on the southeast.

121. **Toorkmuns.** A branch of the Turkish race found in northern Persia and Afghanistan.

122. **Tukas,** from Ader-baijan. **Salore,** a district far south of the Oxus, on the northern border of modern Persia.

123. **Attruck,** a river that empties into the Caspian Sea on the east side.

## NOTES

**128. Ferghana,** a Khanate north of Bokhara.

**129. Jaxartes,** now the Sir Daria. It rises in the Pamere plateau and flows to the north, emptying into the Aral Sea on the east side.

**131. Kipchak,** a Khanate on the Oxus below Khiva.

**132. Kalmucks,** a nomadic tribe of western Siberia. **Kuzzaks,** now called Cossacks.

**133. Kirghizzes,** nomadic Tartars of northern Turkestan.

**138. Khorassan,** region of the sun, a province of northeastern Persia.

**156. corn,** grain. Only in America is the word restricted to Indian corn or maize.

**160. Cabool,** an important city, capital of northern Afghanistan.

**161. Indian Caucasus,** a mountain range which forms the boundary between Afghanistan and Turkestan.

**178–183.** Compare the conduct of Achilles in the *Iliad*, Book I.

**199. sate,** obsolete and poetic for *sat*.

**217.** The brothers **Iran** and **Tur** were the legendary ancestors of the Iranians (Persians) and Turanians (Tartars).

**223. Kai Khosroo,** a famous king of Persia who has sometimes been identified with Cyrus the Great. According to the Persian epic *Shah-Namah*, Sohrab's encounter occurred not in the reign of Kai Khosroo, but in that of his grandfather Kai Kaoos.

**230.** Cf. ll. 609–611.

**232. snow-hair'd Zal.** Tradition relates that Zal was born with snow-white hair. He was exposed as a babe on the loftiest peak of the Elburz mountains (see note, l. 113), but was preserved and cared for by the griffin Simurgh. (See l. 679).

**237–241.** Note here and elsewhere in the poem the device of a number of lines beginning with *And*.

**264–270.** Cf. the account of the arming of Achilles. *Iliad*, XIX.

**270.** Other famous horses of history and poetry are Achilles' Xanthus, Alexander's Bucephalus, the Cid's Babiecca. Don Quixote's Rosinante is a burlesque of these.

**302–308.** One of the few similes which is modern.

**328.** Note the alliteration marking the antithesis.

**347. muse,** wonder.

**379. on his feet.** What force have these words here?

**406–407. sharp rang—***rang sharp*. An inverted repetition, a Miltonic device.

**452. autumn-star,** Sirius, the dog star.

**481. unnatural,** because between father and son.

**481–490.** Cf. Book III, ll. 465–469 of the *Iliad*.

## NOTES

**489.** The Oxus is recalled to our minds throughout the poem. Cf. l. 508.

**497. shore,** archaic form for *sheared*.

**508. curdled,** thickened as with fear.

**516. Rustum!** This cry and its consequences is an invention of Arnold's. In the Persian poem Rustum prayed to the gods, and was awarded success on the third day because of his piety.

**590. my mother.** The Tartar princess, Tahmineh. Her grief at Sohrab's death is treated at length in the Persian poem.

**596. bruited up,** noised abroad.

**613. style,** name, title.

**658–660.** This is Arnold's invention. In the Persian original, Sohrab wears an onyx amulet.

**679. griffin,** an imaginary animal, half lion and half eagle. See l. 232, and note.

**687. proper,** own, peculiar.

**717. found,** ellipsis for *found him*.

**736. caked,** hardened.

**753. Helmund,** a river that intersects Seistan.

**763–4. Moorghab, Tejend,** and **Kohik,** rivers of Turkestan, which are lost in the deserts south of Bokhara.

**765 The northern Sir,** the Sir Daria or Jaxartes. See note, l. 129.

**830. on that day.** Kai Khosroo and a number of his nobles retired to a place far to the north, where the king died. His nobles perished in a tempest while returning to Persia. Arnold makes Sohrab predict Rustum's death with these Persian peers; but this is contrary to the Persian story. See note to l. 223.

**861. Jemshid in Persepolis.** Jemshid, a legendary Persian king who was said to have founded Persepolis, an ancient capital of Persia.

**878. Chorasmia,** the ancient name of Karissan, a once famous empire with about the present limits of Khiva.

**880. Orgunjè,** a village on the Oxus, some seventy miles below Khiva.

**891. new-bathed stars,** just risen out of the sea.

**865–892.** The closing paragraphs turn from the tragedy to the two actors of the busy activities of the armies and the solemn progress of the great river,—to the ceaseless currents of men and nature that must go on unregardful of individual sorrow and suffering.

## NOTES

### THE FORSAKEN MERMAN—(PAGE 33)

In this lovely poem Arnold has related the legend of a mortal maiden who married a merman and then forsook him and her children for human life and "the little gray church on the windy hill." The poem is dramatic in that it is supposed to be spoken, or sung, by the merman as he bids his children to call their last farewell to their mother and descend with him into "the heart of the sea." The merman's strange story has wonderful human pathos, and beautiful descriptions of both the depths of the sea and of "the white-walled town." Still more beautiful perhaps is the exquisite way in which Arnold has varied and suited the meter to the changing emotions of the narrative.

**129. heaths starr'd with broom.** The yellow flower of the broom plant, common in England, is like a star. Cf. the "gold flowered broom" of *Callicles's Song*, p. 87, l. 24.

### SWITZERLAND—(PAGE 37)

"Meeting," "Isolation—To Marguerite," and "To Marguerite —Continued" are the first, fourth, and fifth of a series of seven poems grouped under the title, *Switzerland*.

### ISOLATION—(PAGE 38)

**20.** Cynthia, the moon, according to the myth, kissed Endymion, a mortal in love with her. Cf. any classical dictionary under *Endymion*.

### PHILOMELA—(PAGE 40)

For the Greek myth referred to in the poem, see any classical dictionary under *Philomela*. The myth was located in Daulis (l. 27), a city of Phocis, through which flows the stream Cephisus (l. 27). The poem should be compared with others on the Nightingale by Coleridge, Wordsworth, and Keats. It is in unrhymed verse like *The Future* (p. 53) and *Rugby Chapel* (p. 80).

### DOVER BEACH—(PAGE 42)

One of the best known of the poems in which Arnold gave expression to his moods of religious scepticism and longing. Compare it with *A Summer Night* (p. 48).

## BACCHANALIA; OR, THE NEW AGE—(PAGE 43)

The careful structure of this poem is characteristic of Arnold. In the first division we have (*a*) the evening quiet after the day's work; (*b*) the dance of the Bacchanalians; and (*c*) the dissatisfaction of the shepherd with the revellers and his longing for quiet. In the second division these movements are paralleled by (*a*) the quiet seclusion of an epoch; (*b*) the rush of the new age; and (*c*) the poet's dissatisfaction with the new and his longing for the past. The same thought is given expression in *The Future* (p. 53). Here, as Professor Saintsbury has noted, the idea is clothed with poetic humor "And, like all poetic humour, it oscillates between cynicism and passion, almost bewilderingly. . . . In the first place, note the metrical structure, the sober level octosyllables of the overture changing suddenly to a dance-measure which, for a wonder in English, almost keeps the true dactylic movement. How effective is the rhetorical iteration of

> The famous orators have shone
> The famous poets sung and gone,

how perfect the sad contrast of the refrain—

> Ah! so the quiet was!
> So was the hush!

how justly set and felicitously worded the rural picture of the opening! how riotous the famous irruption of the New Ages! how adequate the quiet moral of the end, that the Past is as the Present, and more also!"

## SELF-DEPENDENCE—(PAGE 47)

One of several poems in which Arnold urges us to seek relief from our discontents in the example of nature. Compare it with the following poem, *A Summer Night*.

## THE FUTURE—(PAGE 53)

One of Arnold's most successful unrhymed poems; well known because of the fine eloquence of the two concluding stanzas.

**36. Rebekah,** Genesis xxiv.

## THE SCHOLAR-GIPSY—(PAGE 56)

This and the four following poems are grouped in Arnold's works as "Elegiac Poems." *The Scholar-Gipsy* and *Thyrsis* are companion poems, both elegies, both pastorals modelled to some extent on Theocritus. Both discuss an escape from this "disease of modern life," and both describe scenes in the country about Oxford. Arnold's note to the poem gives his source for the story of the scholar-gipsy.

"There was very lately a lad in the University of Oxford, who was by his poverty forced to leave his studies there; and at last to join himself to a company of vagabond gipsies. Among these extravagant people, by the insinuating subtilty of his carriage, he quickly got so much of their love and esteem as that they discovered to him their mystery. After he had been a pretty while exercised in the trade, there chanced to ride by a couple of scholars, who had formerly been of his acquaintance. They quickly spied out their old friend among the gipsies; and he gave them an account of the necessity which drove him to that kind of life, and told them that the people he went with were not such impostors as they were taken for, but that they had a traditional kind of learning among them, and could do wonders by the power of imagination, their fancy binding that of others: that himself had learned much of their art, and when he had compassed the whole secret, he intended, he said, to leave their company, and give the world an account of what he had learned."—GLANVIL'S *Vanity of Dogmatizing*, 1661.

Joseph Glanvil (1636–1680) was a writer on philosophical and religious subjects who defended belief in witchcraft. He is alluded to several times in the poem.

**2. wattled cotes.** Sheepfolds. Cf. Milton's *Comus*, l. 344.

**19. corn,** i.e., grain.

**30. Oxford towers.** There are frequent allusions in the poem to places about Oxford, especially in the region of the Cumner (or Cumnor) range of hills, several miles to the south and west. Hurst (l. 57) is Cumnor Hurst, one of these hills. Bablockhithe (l. 74), Fyfield (l. 83), and North and South Hinksey (l. 125) are all hamlets in the Cumnor region. Bagley Wood is beyond South Hinksey. Wychwood Forest (l. 79) is farther to the northwest. Berkshire (l. 58) is the county south of Oxford.

**42. erst,** formerly.

**95. lasher pass,** mill race. The *lasher* is the dam or weir.

**129. Christ Church hall,** one of the most famous buildings of Oxford University.

**208–209.** See the *Æneid* VI, 450–476.

**231.** Of the last two stanzas Mr. R. H. Hutton says:

*NOTES* **95**

"Nothing could illustrate better than this passage Arnold's genius and his art. . . . His whole drift having been that care and effort and gain and pressure of the world are sapping human strength, he ends with a picture of the old-world pride and daring, which exhibits human strength in its freshness and vigor. . . . I could quote poem after poem which Arnold closes by some such buoyant digression: a buoyant digression intended to shake off the tone of melancholy, and to remind us that the world of imaginative life is still wide open to us."

**232. Tyrian trader.** Tyre, the most important city in Phœnicia, was long a chief competitor in the commerce of the Mediterranean.

**238. Chian wine.** Chios, an island in the Ægean sea, was celebrated for its wine.

**244. Midland waters.** The Mediterranean sea.

**245. Syrtes.** Two sandbanks in the Mediterranean, off Africa.

**247. western straits,** Strait of Gibraltar.

**250. Iberia** was an ancient name for Spain.

## THYRSIS—(PAGE 64)

Throughout this poem there is reference to the preceding poem, *The Scholar-Gipsy*, to which it is the companion piece. *Thyrsis* should be compared with Milton's *Lycidas* and Shelley's *Adonais*, two other great elegies, written like this on the model of Theocritus. Here the pastoral element is more prominent than in *The Scholar-Gipsy*. As in *Lycidas* and *Adonais*, the poet's friend is described as a fellow shepherd; and he is given the name Thyrsis, found in Theocritus' Idyls, Vergil's Eclogues, and in later pastoral poetry. The poem also contains, as the notes indicate, allusions to the classical idyls. Yet the classical framework is slight. The birds and flowers and hills are English; and the scene is the same as in *The Scholar-Gipsy*, the country about Oxford. The two Hinkseys (l. 2), the Ilsey Downs in Berkshire (l. 14), and the Fyfield tree (l. 106) are all mentioned in the earlier poem; and the White Horse Vale (l. 15), Ensham and Sanford (l. 109), and the Wytham flats (l. 125) are places within a few miles of Oxford. The poem was finished in 1866 and published in the following year, and marked the virtual end of Arnold's poetic writing. In a letter of April, 1866, to his mother, he speaks of *Thyrsis* as follows:

"Tell dear old Edward [Arnold] that the diction of Thyrsis was modelled on that of Theocritus, whom I have been much reading during the two years this poem has been forming itself, and that I meant the diction to be so artless as to be almost heedless. However, there is a mean which must not be passed, and before I reprint this I will consider well all objections. The images are all from actual observation. . . . The cuckoo in the wet June morning, I heard in the garden at Woodford, and all those three stanzas which you like are reminiscences of Woodford. Edward has, I think, fixed on the two stanzas I myself like best: 'O easy access,' 'And long the way appears,' but that is because they bring certain places and moments before me. . . . It is probably too quiet a poem for the general taste, but I think it will stand wear."

Arthur Hugh Clough (1819–1861) was a poet whose early death cut short the full achievement that his genius promised. He was a student at Oxford with Arnold, and the two shared the same doubts, hopes, and ideals. Clough's verse, like Arnold's, often turned from the simpler human themes he preferred to deal with to subjects of religious doubt and struggle. And he was always restless for an active and practical, rather than a purely literary life. His poems have a singular attractiveness in their revelation of his personality. His character was a most lovable one, and his loyalty to truth invincible, and, like Arnold's gipsy, he lived and died,

> Still nursing the unconquerable hope,
> Still clutching the inviolable shade.

There is a beautiful appropriateness in the plan of the poem which permits Arnold to mourn his dead friend as one worthy of commemoration with Bion, Lycidas, and Adonais, and as the companion of Oxford rambles and early hopes, and as a spirit beset by modern difficulties who nevertheless loyally sought "a fugitive and gracious light, shy to illumine."

**19.** Compare Arnold's famous apostrophe to Oxford in the preface to his *Essays in Criticism*, vol. I (1865).

**35. Shepherd pipe,** in pastoral verse always symbolic of song and poetry.

**80. Corydon,** a shepherd in the Idyls of Theocritus, who competes for a prize in music.

**84. Bion,** a pastoral poet of the second century B.C., whose death was lamented in an Idyl by his pupil, Moschus.

**85.** The ferry over which Charon took the shades of the dead to Hades.

**86–90.** Orpheus by the charm of his lyre persuaded Pluto to restore his wife Eurydice to life. This, however, was on condition that she walk behind her husband, who was not to look at her until they had passed out of the lower regions. Orpheus looked back, and Eurydice was caught back into Pluto's realm. Cf. *Memorial Verses*, 34–39.

**88. Proserpine,** wife to Pluto, was honored in Sicily as the goddess of the spring.

**94-95. the Dorian water's gush divine.** The river Alpheus in the Peloponnesus flows underground for a part of its course. In the Greek myth it was supposed to rise again, as the fountain of Arethusa, in Sicily, in the vale of Enna, the haunt of Proserpine. She was gathering flowers in the vale of Enna when carried off by Pluto.

**167. Arno-vale.** The valley of the Arno in Italy, in which Florence is located, where Clough is buried.

**177. The great Mother,** Ceres, the earth goddess.

**181-190.** Daphnis, the ideal Sicilian shepherd of Greek pastoral poetry, was said to have followed into Phrygia his mistress Piplea, who had been carried off by robbers, and to have found her in the power of the king of Phrygia, Lityerses. Lityerses used to make strangers try a contest with him is reaping corn, and to put them to death if he overcame them. Hercules arrived in time to save Daphnis, took upon himself the reaping contest with Lityerses, overcame him, and slew him. The Lityerses-song connected with this tradition was, like the Linus-song, one of the early, plaintive strains of Greek popular poetry, and used to be sung by the corn reapers. Others traditions represented Daphnis as beloved by a nymph, who exacted from him an oath to love no one else. He fell in love with a princess, and was struck blind by the jealous nymph. Mercury, who was his father, raised him to heaven, and made a fountain spring up in the place from which he ascended. At this fountain the Sicilians offered yearly sacrifices. See Servius, *Comment. in Vergil. Bucol.*, V, 20, and VIII, 68. [Arnold's Note.]

## MEMORIAL VERSES—(PAGE 72)

Wordsworth died on April 23, 1850. These verses are dedicated to his memory. Cf. Arnold's " Essay on Wordsworth."

**17. The iron age,** in classic mythology, the last of the four great ages, and characterized by oppression and misery.

**34-39. Orpheus.** See note to Thyrsis, l. 88.

**72. Rotha,** a small stream that flows by Rydal Mount, where Wordsworth was buried.

## A SOUTHERN NIGHT—(PAGE 75)

In memory of the author's brother, William Delafield Arnold, Director of Public Instruction in the Punjab, and author of *Oakfield, or Fellowship in the East,* who died at Gibraltar on his way home from India, April the 9th, 1859.—[From Arnold's Note.]

## RUGBY CHAPEL—(PAGE 80)

This poem was written in memory of Arnold's father, the famous head-master of Rugby, Dr. Thomas Arnold (1795-1842). In addition to his work as a great teacher, he was an historian, the author of an extensive *History of Rome*, and was Regius Professor of History at Oxford at the time of his death. He was buried in the chancel of Rugby Chapel. The poem is in unrhymed verse like *The Future* (p. 53) and it also has resemblances to that poem in its general view of life.

## CALLICLES'S SONG—(PAGE 87)

From Arnold's drama, *Empedocles on Etna*. Callicles is a young harp player, who remains below on the mountain while Empedocles plunges into the crater. This song by Callicles, who is ignorant of Empedocles' death, concludes the drama.

24. Cf. *The Forsaken Merman*, l. 129.